Frank Tannenbaum as a visitor to Sing Sing Penitentiary in 1916
Source: Archives of the University Seminars at Columbia University

Matt Yeager has written a wonderful history of the life and times of the United States' first convict criminologist, Frank Tannenbaum. Sorting through the publications and archival papers and letters by, to, and about Tannenbaum from the second decade of the twentieth century until his death in 1969, Yeager captures the heart and soul of one of America's early public intellectuals whose critique of the American penal and criminal justice system in the 1920s and 1930s is as valid today as it was when he first presented and published his ideas. Contemporary criminologists, critical and mainstream alike, will all benefit from reading a rare and fascinating book length treatment of a true pioneer in the study of crime and punishment. Tannenbaum who has often been ignored, if not forgotten, by those criminologists who came after him, has now been resurrected in the annals of criminology thanks to the splendid efforts of Yeager.

Gregg Barak, *Eastern Michigan University*

FRANK TANNENBAUM

Frank Tannenbaum and the Making of a Convict Criminologist is a historical biography about Columbia University professor Frank Tannenbaum and his contribution to American criminology. Tannenbaum was a major figure in criminology in the early twentieth century, and is known for his contributions to labeling theory, particularly his conception of the "dramatization of evil" presented in his 1938 book, *Crime and Community.* Tannenbaum served a year on Blackwell's Island penitentiary in New York City for labor disturbances in 1914 and subsequently became a prison reformer, writing about his experiences with the American penal system and serving as the official reporter for the Wickersham Commission's Study on Penal Institutions, Probation, and Parole in 1931. This book explores his unique early career and his influence on convict criminology, drawing on his personal papers housed at the Butler Library at Columbia University.

Matthew G. Yeager is associate professor in the Department of Sociology at King's University College, which is part of Western University in Canada. He obtained his bachelor's degree in criminology from the University of California at Berkeley in 1972 and a master's degree in criminal justice from the State University of New York at Albany in 1975. After spending the next 30 years working as a clinical criminologist and prisoners' advocate in various courts and prisons across North America, Yeager finished a doctorate in sociology from Carleton University, Ottawa, Canada in 2006. He is the author of more than forty articles, covering topics such as offender recidivism, state crime, organized crime, and historical studies. He lives with his family in London, Ontario.

Readers are kindly directed to the following website, which contains further legal materials related to the application and appeal for access to the Tannenbaum adoption files, including the forthcoming decision by the First Appellate Division of the New York State Supreme Court: http://yeager.kingsfaculty.ca/

ROUTLEDGE ADVANCES IN CRIMINOLOGY

1 FAMILY LIFE AND YOUTH OFFENDING
Home is Where the Hurt is
Raymond Arthur

2 CHINA'S DEATH PENALTY
History, Law, and Contemporary Practices
Hong Lu and Terance D. Miethe

3 THE POLITICS OF ANTISOCIAL BEHAVIOUR
Amoral Panics
Stuart Waiton

4 HOOKED
Drug War Films in Britain, Canada, and the United States
Susan C. Boyd

5 THE VIOLENCE OF INCARCERATION
Edited by Phil Scraton and Jude McCulloch

6 VIOLENCE, PREJUDICE AND SEXUALITY
Stephen Tomsen

7 BIOLOGY AND CRIMINOLOGY
The Biosocial Synthesis
Anthony Walsh

8 GLOBAL GAMBLING
Cultural Perspectives on Gambling Organizations
Edited by Sytze F. Kingma

9 SOCIAL CLASS AND CRIME
A Biosocial Approach
Anthony Walsh

10 SECURITY AND EVERYDAY LIFE
Edited by Vida Bajc and
Willem de Lint

11 WOMEN AND HEROIN ADDICTION IN CHINA'S
CHANGING SOCIETY
Huan Gao

12 COLONIAL DISCOURSE AND GENDER IN
U.S. CRIMINAL COURTS
Cultural Defenses and Prosecutions
Caroline Braunmühl

13 EUROPEAN DEVELOPMENTS IN CORPORATE
CRIMINAL LIABILITY
Edited by James Gobert and Ana-Maria Pascal

14 THE MYTH OF MORAL PANICS
Sex, Snuff, and Satan
Bill Thompson and Andy Williams

15 DRUGS AND POPULAR CULTURE IN THE AGE
OF NEW MEDIA
Paul Manning

16 CRIMINAL JUSTICE IN INTERNATIONAL SOCIETY
Edited by Willem de Lint, Marinella Marmo,
and Nerida Chazal

17 AMERICAN SMUGGLING AS WHITE COLLAR CRIME
Lawrence Karson

18 YOUNG MEN AND DOMESTIC ABUSE
David Gadd, Claire L. Fox, Mary-Louise Corr,
Steph Alger and Ian Butler

19 FRANK TANNENBAUM: THE MAKING OF A
CONVICT CRIMINOLOGIST
Matthew G. Yeager

FRANK TANNENBAUM

The Making of a Convict Criminologist

Matthew G. Yeager

Routledge
Taylor & Francis Group
NEW YORK AND LONDON

First published 2016
by Routledge
711 Third Avenue, New York, NY 10017

and by Routledge
2 Park Square, Milton Park, Abingdon, Oxon, OX14 4RN

Routledge is an imprint of the Taylor & Francis Group,
an informa business

© 2016 Taylor & Francis

The right of Matthew G. Yeager to be identified as author of this work
has been asserted by him in accordance with sections 77 and 78 of the
Copyright, Designs and Patents Act 1988.

All rights reserved. No part of this book may be reprinted or reproduced or
utilised in any form or by any electronic, mechanical, or other means, now
known or hereafter invented, including photocopying and recording, or in
any information storage or retrieval system, without permission in writing
from the publishers.

Trademark notice: Product or corporate names may be trademarks or
registered trademarks, and are used only for identification and explanation
without intent to infringe.

Library of Congress Cataloging-in-Publication Data
A catalog record for this book has been requested

ISBN: 978-1-138-93996-7 (hbk)
ISBN: 978-1-315-65254-2 (ebk)

Typeset in Times New Roman
by Apex CoVantage, LLC

Printed and bound in the United States of America by Publishers Graphics,
LLC on sustainably sourced paper.

CONTENTS

	List of figures	x
	Preface	xii
	Acknowledgments	xv
1	American Criminal Justice a Century Hence	1
2	Early Years in New York City	5
3	Arrested as a Wobbly	11
4	Jail: One Year on Blackwell's Island	25
5	Frank's Association with Thomas Mott Osborne	38
6	Prison Work, Prison Reform, Prison Labor	57
7	Becoming a Public Intellectual	72
8	Crime and the Community	83
9	Frank's Contribution to Convict Criminology	98
	Appendix	106
	References	132
	Index	142

FIGURES

	Frank Tannenbaum as a visitor to Sing Sing Penitentiary in 1916	i
	Frank's official 1950s university photo at Columbia	xii
1.1	Total state and federal prison populations, 1978–2013	2
1.2	Sentenced state and federal prison admissions and releases and year-end sentenced prison population, 1978–2012	2
1.3	U.S. State and Federal prison population, 1925–2013	4
3.1	Late nineteenth century etching of Blackwell's Island Penitentiary from the East River, New York City	23
4.1	A pre-1900 etching of Blackwell's Island Penitentiary	25
4.2	An etching of meal time at Blackwell's Island Penitentiary, likely around 1878	26
4.3	Inmates at Blackwell's Island Penitentiary preparing for their breakfast, 1875	29
4.4	A photo of Esther Abramson fishing in the 1920s	36
4.5	An early 1930's photo of Esther Abramson and her two children, Zalkind and Sara Ness	37
5.1	Frank on one of his visits to Sing Sing Penitentiary in 1916, most likely as a guest inmate	39
5.2	1916 photo of Frank with Warden Thomas Mott Osborne at Sing Sing Penitentiary	40
5.3	October 1913 photo of Thomas Mott Osborne posing as an inmate at Auburn Penitentiary	41
7.1	Frank's official 1940s university photo at Columbia	80
7.2	Frank's official 1938 photo as a new professor at Columbia University	81

FIGURES

8.1 Frank Tannenbaum in his Columbia University office,
     circa 1950   88
8.2 A young Jane Belo before her marriage to Frank
     Tannenbaum in 1940   96
9.1 One of Frank's favorite photographs, relaxing at the cottage   104

PREFACE

Frank's official 1950s university photo at Columbia

In the history of criminological thought, particularly its American version, we sometimes forget the contribution of historical figures, especially in the context of the current crisis of mass imprisonment, capital punishment, and even the crimes of the powerful. Frank Tannenbaum is not a name that readily comes to mind among most students of crime. When I was attending the School of Criminology at the University of California, Berkeley beginning in 1970, Tannenbaum was not mentioned, not even in courses on corrections or gang delinquency. Among some criminologists, he is probably best known for his book *Crime and the Community* (1938: 19–20) and his oft-cited quotation concerning the dramatization of evil, an early precursor to labeling theory (Jacoby, 1979):

> The process of making the criminal, therefore, is a process of tagging, defining, identifying, segregating, describing, emphasizing, making conscious and self-conscious; it becomes a way of stimulating, suggesting, emphasizing, and evoking the very traits that are complained of.

Equally interesting was Tannenbaum's view of criminological positivism. "The assumption that crime is caused by any sort of inferiority, physiological or psychological, is here completely and unequivocally repudiated" (p. 22). Tannenbaum reached these conclusions not solely on the basis of his academic research, but because he had been convicted and jailed in his early 20s and had spent time among the so-called dangerous classes.

This is an effort to resurrect the work of a long-ago convict criminologist who had important things to say about the origins of crime and penology. It relies on the body of published work by Frank Tannenbaum himself, much of which is not well known, as well as the Tannenbaum Papers (100 boxes) housed at Columbia University. A separate collection of Tannenbaum materials was also found in the basement archives of the University Seminars Office at Columbia University. In addition, I obtained a copy of Tannenbaum's relatively small FBI file (24 pages) under the Freedom of Information and Privacy Act, 5 U.S.C. 552/552a. A further search was conducted of old New York City police files (there were none), and a Freedom of Information request was made to the New York City Department of Corrections for old prison records (none exist). I also traveled to the University of Syracuse to view the papers of the late Thomas Mott Osborne, the noted American prison reformer. I was ably assisted by retired New York City archivist, Bruce Abrams, in my search for municipal documents pertaining to Frank Tannenbaum. Research was also conducted at the main New York Public Library, the Tamiment Library at New York University, the Center for Jewish History, and the New York Historical Society library, among others.

Finally, I was grateful to obtain the permission of Frank Tannenbaum's nephew, Sherman Tannenbaum, to reproduce the photographs in this monograph. Frank's granddaughter, Annette Hurwitz Jenner, provided a wealth of background data on her father, Zalkind; her aunt, Nessa; and her adoptive grandparents, Esther and Eliahu Hurwitz.

As for methodological innovation, we filed what might be the first petition to unseal adoption court files in the state of New York for historical research purposes. On September 18, 2014, Madam Surrogate Justice Nelida Malave-Gonzalez ruled that I was not entitled to unseal 1931 adoption files involving Frank's two children in order to obtain additional social history information from these archival records. This was despite the fact that all parties to the adoption, including the children, were deceased, and despite written permissions by a surviving nephew and niece permitting me to access these adoption records. Pursuant to the Domestic Relations Law (DRL) for the state of New York, the surrogate ruled that I was not entitled to the records because I was a third party unconnected to the parties to the adoption, and because I had allegedly failed to put forth a "concrete and compelling need" under the "good cause" doctrine to unseal these records. In her view, the archival status of the records did "not support unsealing. Otherwise, the statute's requirement of good cause would become a nullity and adoption records could be unsealed after the mere passage of time…" (In the Matter of the Adoption of Children whose first names are Zalkind and Sara, 2014).

On October 16, 2014, we filed an appeal of this decision with the First Appellate Division of the Supreme Court for the state of New York. We first argued that Madam Surrogate Malave-Gonzalez erred in citing my third-party status, inasmuch as the DRL does not bar such status. It only required that good cause be shown. In our appeal, we further argued that there is historical value in these archival records in the research on a biography of Frank Tannenbaum as a convict criminologist, and that this interest constitutes a public good or public interest, which comes under the "good cause" doctrine of the statute. Finally, we argued that the confidentiality aspects of the statute cannot apply here because the parties to the adoption actually knew each other, they are all now deceased, and consents have been obtained from living relatives.

This matter is pending and a decision is expected sometime in 2016.

ACKNOWLEDGMENTS

> The publisher would like to thank Victor E. Kappeler for his efforts
> in bringing this project forward for the now-defunct Elsevier series
> on theoretical criminology. We appreciate his work in encouraging
> Matthew G. Yeager and helping to shape this important work.

This project took form in 2008, when I obtained some research funds to travel to Columbia University and see a small portion of the Frank Tannenbaum Papers housed at the Butler Library. In 2011, I published a short article about Tannenbaum in *The Prison Journal.* During a recent sabbatical, the project developed into a full-blown monograph on this early American convict criminologist.

I would like to thank my wife, Carolyn Hallett, and our young son, Eli, as we spent his entire ninth grade in New York City while I researched and wrote this book. I was fortunate to be a visiting scholar at Columbia's historic Department of Sociology for the academic year, which enabled me to devote my full attention to this project.

I would like to thank Ms. Jocelyn K. Wilk, public services archivist with the Columbia University Archives and Rare Book and Manuscript Library at the Butler Library on campus. Also assisting was Ms. Tara C. Craig, reference services supervisor. A special thanks is due to Thai Jones, Ph.D., the Herbert H. Lehman Curator for American History at the Rare Book and Manuscript Library. Himself an accomplished historian, Thai has also written about Frank Tannenbaum.

A special appreciation is extended to the original series editor, Victor Kappeler of Eastern Kentucky University, for his sponsorship of this project as part of Anderson Publishing Company's theoretical criminology series. Subsequently, Anderson Publishing was purchased by Taylor & Francis Group. Hence, I was greatly assisted by editor Pamela

Chester, Ph.D. at Routledge Publishing, a division of Taylor and Francis Group, UK.

Finally, I would like to thank my colleagues and the board of directors at King's University College, Western University in Canada, for giving me this opportunity to take a sabbatical and engage in this most fruitful project.

1

AMERICAN CRIMINAL JUSTICE
A CENTURY HENCE

It has now been over a century since Frank Tannenbaum was jailed at Blackwell's Island Penitentiary in New York City. In writing a social history of American criminological thought featuring Tannenbaum, the question arises what has happened to criminal justice in the United States since then, and does this long-forgotten convict criminologist have anything meaningful to say about current trends and controversies? Why delve into the life and times of Frank Tannenbaum if his views are no longer relevant to the issues confronting citizens today? What, then, are some of these trends that Tannenbaum may have addressed some 100 years ago?

Tannenbaum would have been shocked at the explosion of prisoners in the United States since his passing in 1969 (Figure 1.3). Data collected as early as 1925, when approximately 100,000 individuals were confined to state and federal prisons, have now ballooned to approximately 1.5 million prisoners, not counting those held in local county jails. With the addition of local jail populations, this figure is now approximately 2.2 million persons incarcerated (Glaze & Kaeble, 2014).

In terms of rates of incarcerated prisoners per 100,000 U.S. residents, this has pushed the figure to an astounding 700 inmates/100,000 population in the year 2013, putting the United States on par with countries like South Africa and the former Soviet Union. In addition, this means that at any given time, there were approximately 4.7 million convicts being supervised in the community on either probation or parole in 2013. Each year in the United States, about 623,000 inmates are released from state and federal prisons, excluding local jails (Carson, 2014). The implications for reintegration, employment, voting, and housing for this sizeable population are enormous and are only now being recognized by state and federal authorities. What are we to do with the huge numbers of released convicts each year, especially if the costs of the prison industry are now too exorbitant for many states and counties to bear (see Figure 1.2)?

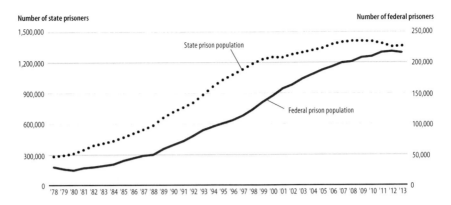

Figure 1.1 Total state and federal prison populations, 1978–2013

Note: Counts based on all prisoners under the jurisdiction of state and federal correctional authorities.

Source: Bureau of Justice Statistics, National Prisoner Statistics Program, 1978–2013.

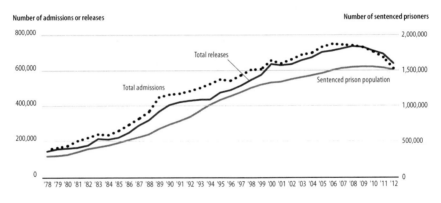

Figure 1.2 Sentenced state and federal prison admissions and releases and year-end sentenced prison population, 1978–2012

Note: Counts based on prisoners with a sentence of more than 1 year. Excludes transfers, escapes, and those absent without leave (AWOL). Includes other conditional-release violators, returns from appeal or bond, and other admissions. Missing data were imputed for Illinois and Nevada (2012) and the Federal Bureau of Prisons (1990–1992).

Source: Bureau of Justice Statistics, National Prisoner Statistics Program, 1978–2012.

This is especially critical when we examine recidivism data—a topic upon which Tannenbaum (1925, 1938) wrote cogently. Recent data from the U.S. government indicate that among thirty states, a whopping 77% of convicts released from state prisons were re-arrested within 5 years of their previous release (Durose, Cooper, & Synder, 2014). Over half were actually returned to the penitentiary within 5 years, and the vast majority of convicts are recommitted on property and drug charges.

Race continues to be one of the defining characteristics of the American correctional system—a topic that Tannenbaum (1924, 1946) wrote upon as well. In 2013, about 550,000 Black inmates were held in state and federal prisons (excluding local jails). Another 332,000 Hispanics were held in confinement, and another 130,000 inmates of aboriginal, Hawaiian, or Pacific Islander background were included. When we compare rates of confinement to those of white inmates per 100,000 population, the ratio of Black, Hispanic, and other inmates is approximately 10:1 (Carson, 2014, Table 8).

One knowledgeable observer has even described this as the New Jim Crow.

> So long as large numbers of African Americans continue to be arrested and labeled drug criminals, they will continue to be relegated to a permanent second-class status upon their release, no matter how much (or how little) time they spend behind bars. The system of mass incarceration is based on the prison label, not prison time.
>
> (Alexander, 2010: 14)

Indeed, the similarities between the penitentiary in America and the Southern slave plantation have not gone unnoticed. As historian Adam Hirsch (1992: 71) has observed:

> One may perceive in the penitentiary many reflections of chattel slavery as it was practiced in the South. Both institutions subordinated their subjects to the will of others. Like southern slaves, prison inmates followed a daily routine specified by their superiors. Both institutions reduced their subjects to dependence on others for the supply of basic human services such as food and shelter. Both isolated their subjects from the general population by confining them to a fixed habitat. And both frequently coerced their subjects to work, often for longer hours and for less compensation than free laborers.

As early as 1923, Tannenbaum was writing about the Ku Klux Klan and Southern prisons, pointing out not only their horrendous conditions (similar to slave plantations), but also the ever-present "color line [which] exists in the prison. The colored population of the Southern prison is predominant. The management is white" (Tannenbaum: 1924: 83).

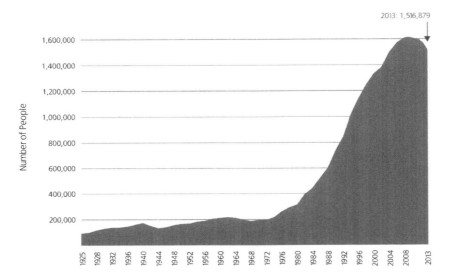

Figure 1.3 U.S. State and Federal prison population, 1925–2013
Source: The Sentencing Project.

This raises the perennial question: What is to be done? According to the latest figures, criminal justice expenditures for corrections in America have now reached $80 billion dollars in fiscal year 2012, 90 percent of which is assumed by state and local governments to the detriment of higher education, social welfare, and public health programs (Kyckelhahn, 2015). Is it really a wise policy to release an inmate with "with $40 in his pocket, sketchy if any identification documents, and no enrollment for basic income support, housing, or health insurance" (Kleiman, Hawken, & Halperin, 2015)?

On the question of alternatives to this massive prison industry, did Frank Tannenbaum have anything to say about the direction of reform, even in the face of a massive infrastructure devoted to cement, steel, and total surveillance? Race, imprisonment, release from confinement, and the future of corrections continue to present themselves as part of the American Dilemma (Myrdal, 1944; Clayton, 1996). Can a long-forgotten figure in North American criminology provide us with some insight and an alternative to a class- and race-based prison gulag?

2

EARLY YEARS IN
NEW YORK CITY

Tannenbaum was one of three children born to Abraham Wolfe Tannenbaum and the former Anna Wilder on March 4, 1893, in a small village called Brod near Galicia, Austria.[1] Both sides of the Tannenbaum family boasted numerous rabbis and other learned people. In fact, Frank was supposed to become a rabbi studying under his grandfather in Galicia, except he ran away every Saturday. This often resulted in a beating administered by an uncle or local rabbi. His own father, Abraham Tannenbaum, was a farmer. In 1899, the elder Tannenbaum left for America without his family to try to establish himself in North Dakota. By December 1904, the rest of the family had joined their father in the United States, settling first in a farm in Great Barrington, Massachusetts, and much later occupying a farm in Sullivan County, New York (Tannenbaum Collection, Box 2, Folder B1, and Box 56).

It is said that Frank's father worked as a subsistence farmer and woodsman, cutting trees for the local lumber mills. The farm did not produce a cash crop, but there were sufficient vegetables and later milk cows to provide food for the Tannenbaum family (Papers of Horace L. Friess, Columbia University, Box 2, Tannenbaum University Seminar file). Several years later, they produced enough cattle to barter for clothes, flour, and farm equipment.

As the eldest child, Frank was expected to do a full day's chores on the farm in addition to his school work. He was bright, a bit mischievous, and learned English quickly. During that first year in America, Frank attended a local, one-room schoolhouse about a mile and a half away, and adored his teacher, a Miss Wetzel. She, in fact, lived with the Tannenbaums. Indeed, it is said that he completed some schooling in Europe from ages 9 through 12, and up to grade seven in two years at Great Barrington (Arciniegas, 1970: 28). Two years later in 1906, following a quarrel with his father, Tannenbaum ran away to New

5

York City to live by himself in a Bowery Hotel for 15 cents a night (Tannenbaum Papers, Box 56. Unpublished manuscript; see Hale, 1995: 216). Economic times were tough, and his father wanted young Frank, then 13 years old, to remain on the farm and forget any further schooling. When Frank announced his intention to go to New York City to pursue an education, his father administered a beating. Shortly thereafter, Frank left on a half-price train ticket with 70 cents in his pocket.

He supported himself as a dishwasher, elevator operator, and waiter. Frank also worked as a bus boy at the Stock Exchange Luncheon Club. He was paid about 15 dollars a month and allowed to scrounge for leftovers in the cellar (unpublished biography, Box 56, bound folder). His best job, however, was as an elevator operator in the Mac Alpern Apartment House, where he had sufficient time to read excerpts from Plato and Ralph Waldo Emerson.

> At that time [age 14], I had a little dingy bedroom on the 5th floor in an East tenement house looking out into a narrow yard. The room was so small that the little table and bed filled it and I had no place for my books excepting under the bed. My bookcase was an old soapbox and everytime I bought a new book, I dragged my soapbox from underneath the bed . . . put my new book in it and . . . took joy in my growing library.

The irony of having to work all day and into the evenings was not lost on Frank. Initially, he was not able to attend school, which was the very reason he ran away to New York City.

Indeed, he never finished high school or graduated from a public school (Box 17, Watson Folder, letter of Jan. 2, 1942, to Harold Graves). In 1909, he became a naturalized American citizen before the King's County Court in Brooklyn (FBI File, 2008). He also developed ties with anarchist Emma Goldman. Indeed, he apparently spent hours in Goldman's office of *Mother Earth*, and in her own biography, she was quite fond of him:

> We all had loved Frank for his wide-awakeness and his unassuming ways. He had spent much of his free time in our office, reading and helping in the work connected with *Mother Earth*. His fine qualities held out the hope that Frank would some day play an important part in the labor struggle. None of us had expected however that our studious, quiet friend would so quickly respond to the call of the hour.
>
> (Goldman, 1931: 523)

EARLY YEARS IN NEW YORK CITY

Even after Tannenbaum was attending Columbia University and had finished his own stint in jail, he wrote to Emma Goldman, who was serving a short sentence (15 days) at the Queens County Jail. In a jailhouse letter to Frank likely written around May 2, 1916, Goldman wrote:

> Indeed, I am not sorry for my 15 days. I know they not only done good to the cause but to myself. Every true rebel needs an occasional sojourn in jail. Of that I am convinced.
>
> (Box 3, Folder G)

Goldman had been convicted for delivering a lecture on birth control (Falk, 2003).

In conjunction with other young students, Frank attended some night classes at the Modern School of the Francisco Ferrer Association. The school was named after Francisco Ferrer y Guardia, a Spanish anarchist and educator who was executed by the state in 1909 (Hale, 1995: 216). One of the ideological mentors of the school was none other than the Russian anarchist Peter Kropotkin, then living in exile in England.

> Kropotkin's hostility to the state, his attack on the corrosive effect of modern industrialism on human dignity, and his search for the ethical, autonomous community undoubtedly provided young Tannenbaum, an informal night student, with key ideas that he carried with him to prison and throughout his life
>
> (Hale, 1995: 219).

Indeed, anarchists were well aware of the conservative tendencies of mainstream education. Hence, they supported the creation of the Modern School in New York City, among others (Berkman, 1910).

As a young boy, Tannenbaum also met and befriended Samuel Roth, whose family also hailed from a shtetl in Galicia, Austria. The two met in 1911 at a meeting of teens interested in entering college (Gertzman, 2013: 28). Indeed, for a period of time, and even while both were accepted at Columbia College in 1916, the two roomed together. Frank, of course, was the political agitator, with his friend Sam the more erudite writer of the two. While attending Columbia as undergraduates, Sam Roth and Tannenbaum started their own magazine called *The Lyric*. It was a magazine of poetry incorporating some of the best emerging work in England and the United States. As World War I approached, Roth unilaterally decided to change the focus of the magazine to a literary journal rather than poetry. Tannenbaum resigned, partly because he disagreed with this decision, and partly because of Roth's intransient and noncooperative approach to editing. *The Lyric* ceased publication in 1917. Nevertheless, the two remained in touch after their days at Columbia, with Roth establishing himself as a provocative publisher of banned European books (*Ulysses* and *Lady Chatterley's Lover*), erotica, and other publications. Roth would serve two federal prison sentences for obscenity and file an unsuccessful case before the U.S. Supreme Court—that only later succeeded in reversing the legal criteria for allegedly obscene material (Gertzman, 2013: xix).

As early as 1913, Tannenbaum was a member of Local 179 of the Industrial Workers of the World (IWW) in Brooklyn, New York City (Hale, 1995: 216). His membership was likely related to a strike organized by the IWW on behalf of restaurant workers in 1912 or 1913 (Avrich, 1995: 216; Saposs, 1926: 153). Frank immersed himself in IWW activities and allegedly "read nothing but the I.W.W." (Jones, 2012: 65). The IWW was an indigenous American labor organization that borrowed some Marxist principles but was clearly more anarchist in orientation. Indeed, the organization was largely estranged from the American socialist party and hostile to the more conservative policies of the American Federation of Labor (Foner, 1965). Tannenbaum later wrote to Daniel Bell that the IWW was critical of and opposed to communism in general (Box 6, Folder B(2), letter to Bell of January 26, 1955). Hence, the IWW largely rejected European Marxist theory and refused to affiliate with the communists (Glazer, 1961).

Late in 1913, Tannenbaum, like many working-class New Yorkers, lost his job.

> Unable to pay for his room at the Sherman Hotel, in the Bowery, he had taken to sleeping in parks and lodging houses. Increasingly, he found himself in 'close contact with the unemployed in New York City.'
>
> (Jones, 2012: 65)

By the winter of 1914, Frank had found a new job as a busboy and was no longer destitute. Still, Tannenbaum was flabbergasted at the treatment the poor received at New York City's Municipal Lodging Home, which was one of the few facilities for the homeless and poor. The stated policy of this city facility was to kick lodgers out at 4:30 in the morning. If they returned more than three times in a month, they were deemed to be vagrants and sent to a workhouse on Blackwell's Island (Holmes, 1914; *The Survey*, 1914).

When not working, Frank spent time at the offices of *Mother Earth*, at the Modern School, or with his fellow IWW members arguing about politics and methods. Indeed, the winter of 1914 was so dire that young Tannenbaum, who was otherwise short, quiet, and conscientious, came up with an idea to help the IWW organize the poor. In January 1914 at an IWW meeting, he proposed leading the unemployed into churches to demand food, lodging, and, most important, paid employment at union wages (Roulston, 1914; Foner, 1965: 444). In theory at least, a key component of this project was to organize the poor under the IWW banner, demand employment and a minimum wage of 30 cents/hour, and a working day of eight hours or less (Survey, 1914).

The harsh winter of 1913–1914 magnified the massive unemployment problem. In New York City alone, it was estimated that at least 300,000 were without work (Hale, 1995: 218). Frank remembers those years as comprising riots and massive unemployment. There were riots in different parts of the United States with men carrying banners that declared, "For Bread or Revolution."

> In New York City, . . . a half million men [were] out of work in the winter of 1913–1914. Thousands of them slept in the parks, alleyways, stood in block-long bread lines, overcrowded the city lodging houses, were packed like herring on the ferry boats where the city tried to make room for them . . .
>
> (Box 56, Tannenbaum bound papers)

Beginning February 27, 1914, Tannenbaum started leading his "Army of the Unemployed" into New York City churches, demanding food and lodging (Folsom, 1991: 205). On March 1, 1914, Frank addressed 300 hungry and unemployed men in Rutgers Square, New York City (Headen, 1937). Frank was quoted as saying:

> We have no scruples as to the law! If it is unlawful to take bread, I refuse to be a law-abiding citizen! A hungry man knows nothing about the law . . . On! Workers of the world. We'll take what we want! . . . Tonight we eat and sleep indoors at the expense of the rich.

His first foray succeeded when he convinced leaders of the First Presbyterian Church to give his motley group 30 cents each. Rev. Duffield and his church deacons felt sorry for Tannenbaum's "Army of the Unemployed" and allotted the entire group, then numbering about

80 persons, the sum of $25. This was sufficient to purchase a meal for all the men and accommodations at the Salvation Army Hotel located in the Bowery (Fowler, 1981: 97). This technique worked at several other locations, during which Tannenbaum exhorted his "Army of the Unemployed" to demand an 8-hour working day and a minimum daily wage of $3 (Maier & Weatherhead, 1974). Until employers saw fit to hire them on these terms, they would march every night upon some church or public institution and stay there until they were fed and housed (Headen, 1937). Naturally, this labor-organizing technique attracted the attention of financial elites, and coverage appeared in the *New York Times*, *New York Evening Post*, *New York Tribune*, and the *New York World*—all of whom were demanding that action be taken to eradicate Tannenbaum and his motley Army of the Unemployed.

Indeed, the editorial of the *New York World* on March 4, 1914 (p. 4), referred to Tannenbaum and his so-called army as a "criminal menace":

> [U]nless energetic measures are used, we may to expect gangs of professional gunmen and thugs to join the professional unemployed in terrorizing public assemblies from the Battery to Harlem . . . The IWW leaders, who are inviting the worst elements of a great city to plunder, do not want work . . . They seek a "social revolution."

Tannenbaum immediately was labeled a wild radical. Francis Perkins, an early social worker and labor secretary under President Franklin D. Roosevelt, (1955; vol.1, part 2, pp. 306–307) remembers Tannenbaum as

> . . . absolutely wild. We didn't have the word "communist" in those days, but he was certainly called everything else. He was wild. The speeches he made rivalled "workers of the world arise." It was "everybody rise and demand." He was quite young and quite illiterate. People got interested in him because he was quite bright—very bright. He took advantage of every opening. He knew how to interview the press.

Note

1 Much of this early history comes from Frank's brother, Louis Tannenbaum, in a questionnaire he filled out on February 21, 1973, for a history later compiled by Weatherspoon and Maier (1974). Cf. Archives, Columbia University Seminars, Folder AY72273. In an interview for the *New York Times*, Frank admitted, "My mother could never remember my birthday. March 4, 1983, is approximate and arbitrary" (Breit, 1951).

3

ARRESTED AS A WOBBLY

On March 4, 1914, the then-conservative *New York Times* reported that Tannenbaum—only 21—led a small army of eighty-three unemployed men into the Roman Catholic Church of St. Alphonsus on West Broadway and demanded food and shelter (*New York Times*, March 5, 1914; Maier & Weatherhead, 1974; Delpar, 1988). In actual fact, Frank and 192 followers were arrested by the police that evening, but only Tannenbaum was charged with forced unlawful entry and inciting to riot, the last being a felony. Ironically, the day was Tannenbaum's birthday, and the *Times* reporter quoted Tannenbaum as saying he intended to celebrate it in "a glorious manner." Newspaper coverage made no reference to violence or the breaking of locks on church doors. When arraigned on charges of unlawful entry and inciting to riot, Magistrate Campbell set bail at $5,000, a figure clearly meant to deny bail to this young Industrial Workers of the World (IWW) organizer (*New York Times,* March 5, 1914, p. 2). Despite pleas from counsel to lower the amount, Magistrate Campbell refused to lower bail. Frank Tannenbaum spent a night in jail. On a renewed motion for bail, Magistrate John Freschi raised bail to $7,500 on March 6, 1914.[1] However, before the Court of General Sessions on March 12, 1914, the bail amount was reduced to $5,000. According to Tannenbaum's own statement at sentencing, he did not make bond or pretrial release and instead refused bail "while the rest of their comrades were in prison" (Orth, 1919: 210; Vorse, 1935: 64).

His arrest and subsequent trial were extensively covered in the press. Indeed, spectators had to be limited to fifty persons, and there were numerous police in attendance to manage a potential crowd, which never materialized during the trial. In selecting the jury, the prosecutor was allowed to ask prospective jurors whether they were members of

"Socialist political parties" like the IWW (*New York Times*, March 25, 1914; Luhan, 1936: 97). As part of the temper of the time, New York City Mayor John Purroy Mitchel warned the IWW that any "general disorder or disturbance of the peace will not be permitted" (*New York Times*, March 25, 1914). He even questioned whether the unemployed led by the IWW were legitimate: "I understand that these people are not rightfully members of that class, for my understanding is that they wouldn't take work if they got it." From the trial and news reports, it became clear that Tannenbaum was arrested on orders from both the police commissioner and mayor. His trial, therefore, had overwhelming political overtones.

Shortly before the trial on Saturday, March 21, 1914, members of the IWW led a march of approximately 1,000 people up 5th Avenue in New York City, clearly challenging elite interests (*New York Times*, March 25, 1914). It was reported that IWW leaders like Emma Goldman and Alexander Berkman were now under political surveillance by New York City red squad detectives "since the beginning of the Tannenbaum demonstrations against the city's churches." Indeed, it was Goldman herself who exhorted her followers during this demonstration to "go to churches, go to the hotels and restaurants, go to the bakeshops, and tell them they must give you something to keep you from starving."

Over the objection of Frank's defense attorney, a police transcript of a speech Tannenbaum gave to homeless men in Rutgers Square alleged that Frank had predicted that blood would be shed (*New York Times*, March 26, 1914). In fact, he had merely agreed with someone in the crowd that blood was shed during the French Revolution. Police officers who were actually stationed at St. Alphonsus Church testified that the "Army of the Unemployed" broke through a locked door of the church.[2] During the trial, about a dozen of the men led into church by Tannenbaum testified on his behalf, indicating there was no disorder and no forced entry. Tannenbaum had asked a priest to let the men sleep in the church pews "on condition that they clean up the premises the next day" (*New York Times*, March 27, 1914). Witnesses for the defense testified that Tannenbaum and his "Army of the Unemployed" were told by the Catholic priest that no shelter or food would be forthcoming. Nevertheless, they were not permitted by the police to exit (Luhan, 1936: 100). The detectives were waiting for instructions from the commissioner's office. Indeed, the radical press reported that while Tannenbaum was negotiating with church elders in the rectory, the police commissioner had ordered additional reinforcements and half a dozen paddy wagons to St. Alphonsus Catholic Church (*New York Call*, Mar. 5, 1914: 2).

IWW leader William D. Haywood was quoted as saying:

> I am not all surprised. The police have followed the tips of the newspapers, which have been continually advising them to get in and do something. The action of the police can be directly laid at the door of the capitalist press, which has been egging the police along to use their power.
>
> The demonstrations in the churches serve a good purpose in that they draw the attention of the public to the terrible number of homeless workers in the city. There has been a general silence on the part of the newspapers regarding the number of unemployed workers, for they did not like to tell the truth.
>
> I think that the general effect of these demonstrations will be that there will be insistence on the part of the people to create work for the men. There are many ways it can be done.
>
> (Ibid.)

Naturally, the socialist press was highly critical of Tannenbaum's arrest and prosecution. In the March 3rd issue of the *New York Call* (1914a: 1–2, 6), it was reported that Tannenbaum led a contingent of 300 unemployed men into St. Mark's Church at the invitation of the pastors. A large meal was prepared, and prior to this quasi-occupation, Tannenbaum gave a rousing speech in Rutgers Square, stating, "[A] starving man was entitled to food." He asserted that, denied work, a jobless man had the right to take necessaries of life in any way that he could get them. Of interest, detectives were observed outside the church and actually were asked to leave by church officials. In an editorial that same day, the newspaper warned: "It is a warning to capitalism. Today, the wild men are marching. Tomorrow they will be singing."

Prior to Tannenbaum's arrest for inciting to riot, he had given a speech that day referring to the IWW's campaign for an 8-hour day and promising that the IWW would station men outside all factories. Clearly, this represented a threat to corporate capital.

Shortly after Tannenbaum's detention, the police started arresting any IWW supporter who had the audacity to address large crowds (*New York Call,* March 6, 1914b: 1–2). Some speakers prevailed, including a fellow IWW member named Joseph D. Carroll, who did not blame the police. "This was put upon the shoulders of Commissioner McKay, who, he asserted, took orders from the merchants and contractors, whose businesses benefit from the existence of a large unemployed army" (*New York Call,* March 7, 1914). Somehow, Tannenbaum had a message smuggled from the Tombs to the gathering. It read as follows:

> To the Boys on the outside: I want to say that you should continue this work we have only just begun, and not cease from your activities until such time as the city has provided the shelterless with shelter, the hungry with food—or given them work under union conditions, and if this is impossible, until such time as it has jailed all men out of work, thus giving them at least a small part of the food and shelter that all human beings are entitled to.
>
> (Ibid., p. 2)

Prior to the trial, the editorial in the March 12th *New York Call* (March, 12, 1914) noted that the felony charge of inciting a riot had collapsed before the grand jury. Instead, Tannenbaum was charged with a misdemeanor of "unlawful assembly." The editorial further charged: "For in the light of common sense, Tannenbaum's real offense was that he was not willing to 'starve to death in a legal and constitutional manner.'" In point of fact, Tannenbaum was officially charged with two misdemeanors—unlawful assembly and disobeying the commands of a police officer.[3]

As the trial opened, most of the so-called "Army of the Unemployed" had their cases dismissed, except for Tannenbaum and a small number of others who received sentences of 30 to 60 days on Blackwell's Island penitentiary. On the advice of his radical colleagues at *Mother Earth* and within the IWW, Tannenbaum elected to go to trial, even if privately he had reservations (see *The Masses,* May 1914, p. 3).

One of the IWW supporters who was sentenced to 60 days in jail was an 18-year-old young man named Isidore Wisotsky, who would later write about this experience. He had emigrated from Russia to New York City with his family circa 1909 at age 14. Wisotsky was a young early member of the IWW and an acquaintance of Frank's who attended the early meetings during which the occupation plan was developed. Wisotsky remembered the early meeting this way:

> Frank Tannenbaum, Ed Lewis, Teddy Freedman and Frank Hamilton addressed the group. At that meeting we decided that the best and most effective protest would be to lay siege on leading institutions and churches and demand food and shelter,

and a warm place to sleep. And once we made our way into churches, we would not abandon our places or desert our posts even if it meant fighting the police and personal arrest. Let the world hear the cry of woe of the hungry.

(Wisotsky, 1978, Chap. V, p. 103)

According to Wisotsky, who was in attendance, Tannenbaum addressed the unemployed men during their occupation at the St. Alphonsus Catholic Church, announcing "We are the victims of the present capitalist order. Society owes us a livelihood. No one of us will leave this place of his own free will." (Wisotsky, 1978: 104) Another member of Tannenbaum's army was Charles Robert Plunkett, who, like Wisotsky, was arrested with Tannenbaum on March 4, 1914. He clearly remembered that the initial idea to occupy the churches was Tannenbaum's (Avrich, 1995: 214). Plunkett received 15 days in jail and even testified at Tannenbaum's trial.

At trial, the facts emerged that Tannenbaum's all-white, male jury was composed largely of businessmen and small tradesmen (*New York Call,* March 25, 1914, p. 3). Evidence at trial indicated that Tannenbaum was met by police detectives at the church and asked to speak with the priests about his "army" entering the church. In the company of the police, Tannenbaum was led into the rectory to talk with the monsignor in charge of St. Alphonsus Church. During cross-examination, it was revealed that detectives had telephoned for additional police officers even before Tannenbaum and his entourage had entered the church building (*New York Call,* March 26, 1914, p. 3).

Testimony from several newsmen who were covering the spectacle indicated that the crowd was neither noisy nor disorderly. In fact, once the men had entered the church proper, while Tannenbaum was negotiating with the priests, the newsmen found themselves unable to leave the church until they showed their "police card" (*New York Call,* March 27, 1914, p. 1). One reporter even testified that "Tannenbaum then turned to the reporters and directed their attention to the fact that he had offered to take the men from the church, and was able and willing to do so. He declared the police would be to blame if any trouble occurred." (p. 2). The rest, including Frank, remained effectively detained within the church while policemen and paddy wagons arrived.

A reporter for the socialist newspaper, the *New York Call* (March 28, 1914, p. 1) wrote that Tannenbaum made a "poor witness" and was perceived as arrogant and lofty before the jury, sometimes with a "sneering, unpleasant smile." While being cross-examined by the prosecutor,

Tannenbaum repudiated Christianity and denied any interest in religion or God. This, according to the reporter, damaged any potential sympathy that may have existed among jurors. It took the jury only 45 minutes to reach their verdict: guilty on both counts. Judge Wadhams then sent the jury back to consider a single-count verdict, and it rendered a guilty verdict to unlawful assembly.

After a 4-day trial for what was then a misdemeanor—unlawful assembly—Tannenbaum was convicted on March 27, 1914. At the end of his trial, Frank insisted on being sentenced immediately and gave a defiant speech at the time of sentencing that was quoted extensively in the newspapers, even in the august *New York Times* (March 28, 1914). In *The Masses* (1914) Tannenbaum wrote:

> I am accused of participating in an unlawful assembly. I don't know of any assembly on the part of the working people that would be unlawful. It was unlawful. Of course, it was unlawful. I don't doubt that.
>
> Why is there all this nonsense about bloodshed? The capitalist class sheds more blood in one year than the workers do in five. We have been killed in the mines, we have been killed in the factories, in buildings, and on the battlefield. We don't fear death, for we have nothing to live for. There has never been a war in the interests of the workers, and yet it is the worker who dies.
>
> I don't believe the Assistant District Attorney has heart enough to be a dog catcher. He did me a great injustice when he said that I took "$25 graft" in the church. It was given to Mr. Martin. We took hungry men—eighty-three in number—to a restaurant and fed them. They talk about religion—praying to God—I know of no better religion than seeing a number of starving men comfortably seated around a clean table eating.
>
> The day that I was brought into the court, justice flew out of the window and never came back. You jurymen never take the circumstances, the passions, the feelings of men into consideration. These boys are more spontaneous, they are more human, I think, than other people, so they can't adapt themselves to this rotten system. It is my last trial. If I am ever arrested again, there will be no more trials. You couldn't get a jury of workingmen to convict me. These gentlemen are members of your class. They are capitalists in miniature.

Judge William H. Wadhams, Court of General Sessions, who sat through the entire trial, rose to the defense of America:

> You have failed to appreciate the spirit of American institutions. Most of those who come here from other countries come to work, to use every means to better their fellow-men. There is no place in the world where the workingman finds such opportunities as in the United States. One who goes to the pier and watches the incoming ships, overcrowded with those who are coming to these shores, realizes that here is the best place in the world for every man who has industry. Your father and mother realized that. They came here and brought their boy with them.

The trial was clearly political and an effort by ruling elites to address proto-revolutionary elements. Judge Wadhams sentenced young Frank Tannenbaum to the maximum sentence: 1 year's incarceration on Blackwell's Island Penitentiary and a fine of $500, "to stand committed one day for each dollar of said fine unpaid."[4] An appeal was contemplated, but never filed, as the legal fees were prohibitive. Nevertheless, his jailing on Blackwell's Island resulted in a virtual "cause célèbre" among radicals. During the evening of March 27, after Tannenbaum had been sentenced, a meeting was held at Rutgers Square during which a resolution was read out loud and passed by those present. According to a reporter from the *New York Call* (March 28, 1914, p. 2), it read as follows:

> Resolved: That we, the unemployed workingmen of New York, assembled tonight at Rutgers Square, rise to protest against the arrest, conviction, and sentence of Frank Tannenbaum, for the following reasons:
> We claim that the arrest was a frame-up, as was proven by the facts:
>
> First, that the newspapers before his arrest called for his arrest.
> Second, that Tannenbaum was requested by one of the officers to come back into the church and remain there until the officers found out what to do.
> Third, that after everybody was requested to leave the church, the officers held the men back, as was shown by a flashlight photograph and that the officers closed and locked the doors.
> Fourth, that the witnesses testified that the officers swore in the church and that the photograph taken shows that the

officers had their hats on in the church themselves, thereby affording convicting evidence against Tannenbaum. Be it therefore

Resolved. That we demand immediate justice be given in the name of humanity.

Emma Goldman wrote to apologize for not visiting him in the Tombs (New York City's famous Manhattan House of Detention). She observed:

I do not know whether the thought of going to churches originated with you, but no matter in whose mind it was born, you have carried out the thought and thereby you have added a most ingenious and courageous peace of work to the revolutionary propaganda.
(Box 4, Folder R, Letter of March 31, 1914)

On his imprisonment, Frank would write a short letter to his parents in upstate New York (Box 5, Folder T(1), undated letter, March 1914):

Dear Folks: I have just been committed to serve 1 year in jail. Don't worry. My friends will take great care of me. I will not be able to write to you, only once in a few months. But when I come out, I will spend some time at home. With regards to all at home, I remain your loving son.

A Reverend Holmes (1914: 94) concluded that Frank had placed the issue of the homeless and unemployed on the front pages of newspapers and "forced ninety millions of people in the United States to know that there is a question of the unemployed, and to ask what can be done about it." Of interest, after Tannenbaum was arrested, several churches actually opened their doors to the unemployed (*The Survey*, 1914; Foner, 1965: 447).

Max Eastman, editor of *The Masses*, devoted the May 1914 issue to "The Tannenbaum Crime," arguing

[w]hat must outrage the moral sense of every man is that after acknowledging the high motive under which Tannenbaum had acted, confessing that there was no selfish purpose, no desire to injure anyone or gain anything for himself, that he was seeking only "to better the condition of his fellow man," Judge Wadhams inflicted upon that boy who had never been in a law court before, what is by the decent customs of the courts reserved for

habitual criminals charged with serious offenses against persons or property, the extreme penalty of the law.

On the early morning of July 4, 1914, while Tannenbaum sat in his cell at Blackwell's Island Penitentiary, a severe explosion literally ripped the top off an apartment complex located on Lexington Avenue in New York City. Four IWW anarchists, including Arthur Caron, were killed instantly. Tannenbaum knew them all through the Modern School and the IWW, and may have dodged a bullet that morning. In fact, Caron had been arrested with Tannenbaum at St. Alphonsus Catholic Church (Flynn, 1955: 190). The police allegedly believed that Caron and his associates were plotting to blow up the residence of John D. Rockefeller in Tarrytown, New York (*New York Times,* July 5, 1914:, p. 1; Jones, 2012). Previously in May, Caron had been arrested in downtown Tarrytown for disorderly conduct—which was essentially a soapbox speech protesting the Ludlow massacre in Colorado and Rockefeller's involvement. In the process, he was beaten by local police officers. While on bail, Caron and Alexander Berkman returned to Tarrytown to give another speech in late June, an affair that resulted in a mini-riot and serious injuries to Caron (Jones, 2012: 227–228).

When Tannenbaum was finally released on March 9, 1915, a reception was held in his honor attended by several hundred people and a rally at Union Square "to welcome Frank Tannenbaum back to the ranks of the I.W.W. agitators" (*New York Times,* March 10, 1915, p. 6; March 14, 1915, sec. 2, p. 10.; *New York Call,* March 10, 1915, p. 3). According to witnesses, he received a 5-minute ovation and proceeded to describe the brutal and inhumane conditions of confinement.

A day earlier, on March 8, 1915, Judge William Wadhams signed an order remitting Tannenbaum's $500 fine on the basis that he was poor, could not afford to pay the fine, and had served his penitentiary sentence in full.[5] He noted in a written decision that

> [t]he defendant professed to act from what appeared to him to be a good motive, namely, to center public attention upon the condition of unemployment, by leading a crowd to a church to demand food and shelter. In so doing, however, he assembled with others in such a manner as to disturb the public peace, participating by his presence, aid and instigation. His was not peaceable assembling with others for lawful purposes of protest and petition.
>
> The evidence which satisfied the jury showed that the assemblage, of which he was a part, swept past the police at the entrance

of St. Alphonsus Church knocking down two women within the church, stumbling over the legs of a worshipper at a shrine near the entrance, crowding a young woman from the aisle and compelling a man engaged in worship to withdraw from his pew to make room, stepping from seat to seat and failing upon request of the priest on the word of the defendant to withdraw.

Nevertheless, Judge Wadhams concluded that the "rich pay and can afford to do so and the poor who cannot, suffer, not for the offense, but because of their poverty." The Office of the District Attorney did not oppose the motion to remit the fine, and the motion was granted permitting Tannenbaum's release the following day.

In an interview reported in the socialist newspaper, the *New York Call,* Tannenbaum was asked, "What does jail do to a man?" (Ureles, 1915). On the very day of his release, Frank was interviewed by several reporters in the offices of *Mother Earth.*

Well, boys, I'll tell you. It makes a criminal in the truest sense of this word out of him. No man . . . who has ever been in jail respects or fears the law. If a man has morals, religion, belief in God and mankind, if he ever believed in the love of humanity, it is crushed out of him in jail . . . Every man who has been in jail has had his self-respect destroyed and every man who leaves jail is an enemy to society.

Well, in a way, this has been one of the richest years of my life. It has enhanced my determination to make this world a better one to live in. It has made me realize that no one can help the worker but himself. It has brought me in contact with a class of men that I could never have known otherwise; it has taught me the fineness and cruelty of man.

I'm not a rationalist . . . I am an industrial unionist morally and socially. I believe the greatest crime a man commits is to starve. I believe the biggest thing in this universe is the human being; the excuse for the universe is that it helps man. It is my belief that a real religion lies not in the sleek, fat priest who raises his eyes to heaven, forgetting the poor who live in a hell on earth, but in the man who throws himself, heart and soul, in an endeavor to help make out of this hell a place to live in.

Later in this interview, Tannenbaum described the beatings that were administered at Blackwell's Island Penitentiary, suggesting that "the jailors are in the main far greater criminals than the prisoners." Little did anyone know that Frank Tannenbaum would devote the first half of his career to critiquing the American prison system and that his viewpoint was informed by the status of being a former convict.

Indeed, right after his welcome-back rally and interview by the news media, Tannenbaum spent the better part of a day on the campus of Columbia University as a guest of various friends and sympathizers. He is reported to have said, "I want to continue my education, which has been interrupted so many times as so many places" (*New York Tribune,* March 11, 1915, p. 4).

On the evening of his release from prison, March 9, Tannenbaum was feted at a celebration of about 500 IWW supporters and anarchists at the Harlem Casino. There he told the assembled that

> I am here to fight the social system that permits men to stand meekly in bread lines begging for food. I want to show those men who are broken in spirit that they have a right to demand work, and I want to show the world that an empty stomach is no excuse for a broken head just because of the tyranny of the police.
>
> (*New York Sun,* March 10, 1915, p. 14)

Just a few days later on March 13, Tannenbaum addressed a throng of 2,000 persons in Union Square, New York City. With police officers looking on, he told the gathering,

> The wife of the unemployed husband should refuse to pay rent until her husband has employment. Don't give what little money you may have to the landlord; save it and buy food. No work, no rent—let that be your motto. Organize and make of yourselfs a menace.
>
> These fine people don't want to solve the problem. They want to throw a bone to you. Mrs. Astor and her ilk give a great party at a cost of $100,000. The charity gets $200. They give you a meal at Christmas time. Do you know what you should do with that meal? Hurl it back in their faces. You don't want charity; you want work.
>
> Organize! If you don't organize, if you don't make it clear that you won't starve, if you don't defy every institution, you'll get nothing.
>
> (*New York Tribune,* March 14, 1915, p. 9)

The demonstration was orderly, and surprisingly, there were no directives from above to arrest Tannenbaum.

He also visited society matron and IWW sympathizer Mabel Dodge Luhan (1936: 115) in the company of Max Eastman,[6] the then-editor of *The Masses.*

> He had kept his eyes open and had learned all there was to be known about *that* prison. He wanted to stick to prisons, he said, wanted to learn more, to improve himself, and then give his life to changing the conditions of prisons in America. He was crystallized in the prison complex.

In fact, right after being released from prison, an anonymous donor provided funds to editor Max Eastman, which allowed the magazine to hire Tannenbaum prior to starting his university studies at Columbia the following year (Tannenbaum Collection, Box 2, Correspondence of Max Eastman, dated 18 May 1915; Maik, 1994: 124–125).

But it was soon thereafter that Frank Tannenbaum showed up at the massive strike at the Standard Oil plant in Bayonne, New Jersey, involving up to 5,000 striking workers. Both the IWW and the more conservative American Federation of Labor were attempting to organize the strikers (*New York Times,* July 22, 1915). There had been violence on the strike line, including at least two fatalities, several strikers wounded by gunshot, and numerous deliberately set fires at the plant. Prominent in this effort were hired "thugs" of John D. Rockefeller's Standard Oil Company (*New York Call,* July 23, 2915, pp. 1, 3). On July 21, 1915, Frank arrived to address the strikers at Mydosch's Hall and to help organize a public funeral for the striker who was killed. Local sheriff Eugene Kincaid supported the position of Standard Oil and tried to get the strikers to return to work, asserting that he, too, favored increased wages and better working conditions. For its part, the company blamed the usual suspects, "professional agitators," for instigating the strike.

The next day, there was further violence between strikers and armed company guards, with the governor of New Jersey calling out the National Guard, which was not activated. Skirmishes, however, broke out between the strikers and even the 250 sheriff deputies called into action. According to the press (*New York Times*, July 24, 2015, p. 5), Tannenbaum had intended to make an "inflammatory speech" during the funeral for one of the strikers, but was told not to appear in town on the threat of arrest. Several days later, Tannenbaum returned to address the strikers on July 26, 1915, and was illegally arrested by the sheriff and assaulted by Kincaid when he continued to address the strikers. The nimble sheriff then proceeded to punch and arrest the chairman of the strike committee and try to take over as strike leader (*New York Times*, July 27, 1915, p. 1, 4), promising the workers a vague increase in their wages.

Indeed, Sheriff Kinkaid eventually settled the strike after nearly 2 weeks of a plant shutdown by marching the workers back into the Standard Oil plant and negotiating a nominal wage increase and promising police protection from company guards (*New York Times*, July 28, 1915). As for Frank, he was released without charges, with the sheriff telling reporters:

> I release you because you're not a liar. You are a truthful man and not afraid to stand up for what you believe. You're a fighter and I like a fighter. It's too bad you cannot turn your abilities to law and order. If you did they would get you somewhere. I am sorry for you, but I admire your grit.
> (*New York Times*, July 29, 1915. p. 18)

Shortly thereafter, Sheriff Kinkaid took a leave of absence due to alleged mental fatigue and left his office in the company of his wife.

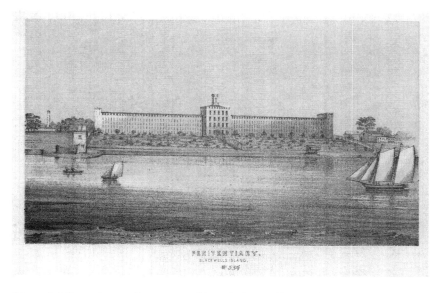

Figure 3.1 Late nineteenth century etching of Blackwell's Island Penitentiary from the East River, New York City

Notes

1 City Magistrate's Court, 10th District, Case No. 98573. Order of Magistrate John Fresdhi, dated March 6, 1914.
2 New York City Municipal Archives, District Attorney file 98573, original complaint by Detective Patrick H. Gildea dated March 4, 1914.
3 Indictment of the Grand Jury of the County of New York, dated March 10, 1914, Case No. 98573, found in the files of the District Attorney for Manhattan, No. 13540.
4 Handwritten notation on Indictment of the Grand Jury of the County of New York, dated March 27, 1914, Case No. 98573, found in the files of the District Attorney for Manhattan, No. 13540.
5 Order of J. Wadhams, dated March 8, 1915, Case No. 98573, found in District Attorney File for Manhattan (No. 13540).
6 It is paradoxical how Tannenbaum's career paralleled that of Max Eastman, himself an early committed American socialist. In his later years, Eastman repudiated Stalinism and even endorsed the market structure of unbridled capitalism (Eastman, 1955).

4
JAIL
One Year on Blackwell's Island

Frank Tannenbaum would later write a series of articles in *The Masses* about his experiences on Blackwell's Island, which eventually led to a formal investigation by the State Commission on Prisons and the resignation of the then warden (Tannenbaum, 1915, 1916). Of interest, after reading Tannenbaum's article in *The Masses*, Richard M. Hurd, then head of the State Commission on Prisons, invited Frank to a meeting at his office located in downtown New York City. Not

Figure 4.1 A pre-1900 etching of Blackwell's Island Penitentiary

surprisingly, Tannenbaum's allegations of inhumane treatment and brutality at Blackwell's Island Penitentiary were initially denied by the commissioner of the New York City Department of Corrections. Nevertheless, Tannenbaum (1915a, 1915b, 1915c, 1916) alleged that he had seen unsafe and unsanitary conditions, including men dying of tuberculosis locked up with healthy, young convicts; sick men working in the bake shop, kitchen, and dining room; blankets never fumigated; and various beatings he either witnessed or could document. He described a penal institution in which visits were highly restricted, inmates smoked "dope" because of being confined to their cells on weekends and holidays, and various petty regulations that were routinely flouted by the inmates. Indeed, Tannenbaum spent 2 months of his sentence in solitary confinement for alleged insolent behavior. During his imprisonment, a riot broke out in the prison, which was violently put down by guards (*New York Times*, July 11, 1914, p. 1.) The *Times*, whose source was prison authorities, quoted New York City Commissioner of Corrections Katharine B. Davis as saying "Order will be maintained in the penitentiary on Blackwell's Island, even if it necessitates the calling out of the militia. You fellows must behave. I'll have it no other way."

Figure 4.2 An etching of meal time at Blackwell's Island Penitentiary, likely around 1878

Tannenbaum was considered one of the ringleaders by Commissioner Davis and her warden, Patrick Hayes, and placed on bread and water in solitary confinement. Reporters were allowed to interview some of the convicts who were in lockdown, and they stated that Warden Hayes was the source of the riot. In fact, the warden wanted to starve the so-called ringleaders, but was overruled by the commissioner, who was quoted as saying, "I don't believe in starvation or thirst. I want the men to get enough food to sustain them and I insist particularly on their having plenty of water" (*New York Times*, July 11, 1914, p. 1).

Frank admitted to reporters that he urged his fellow inmates in the brush shop to strike and practice sabotage (*New York Times*, July 11, 1914, p. 3.) There were reports of privileges taken away by the warden on several ranges of cells for the infractions of a few, convicts being deliberately underfed, and guards routinely using excessive violence against inmates. In the end, the commissioner backed her 70-year-old warden, who was a Civil War veteran, and refused to remove him.

Several days later, the commissioner announced to the press that Frank Tannenbaum apologized for his activities and wished to be released from solitary confinement. He had been kept in the "cooler" on bread and water and was sleeping on the cement floor (*New York Times,* July 14, 1914, p. 5). For his part, Warden Hayes admitted to reporters, "Isn't it funny . . . that you have to starve a prisoner to get anything out of him." But in fact, Tannenbaum was not released by the warden and remained in solitary confinement, allegedly due to his Industrial Workers of the World (IWW) principles that he "stand against authority at all times" (*New York Times*, July 15, 1914, p. 18).

Not surprisingly, Warden Hayes was later the subject of an inquiry in 1915 by the state prison commission. They concluded that Blackwell's Island Penitentiary was in worse condition than Sing Sing, which they had just visited. In his testimony before the commission, Warden Hayes admitted using a water hose to subdue violent prisoners in their cells and locking "prisoners in 'the cooler' on bread and water for days until they promised to behave" (*New York Call,* July 15, 1915, p. 2) He repeatedly denied this was torture.

At this juncture, it is interesting to note the 1915 review of prison conditions by the Prison Association of New York (1916), part of which focused on Blackwell's Island Penitentiary. The census of the prison at Blackwell's Island revealed there were about 1,800 inmates, with 700 double-celled (Prison Association of New York, 1916, p. 424). This was a population of over 60 percent rated capacity at the time. Many of the cells were quite small—a majority of which were only 7 feet, 6 inches by 3 feet, 8 inches. "The faulty system of discipline and the general lack of cooperation between prisoners and authorities is undoubtedly due to the repressive principle upon which the warden of the Penitentiary bases his administration" (Prison Association of New York, 1916, p. 425). The association went on to indict literally every aspect of the prison, from too few cells, unsanitary conditions, and poor conditions, to insufficient hospital accommodations (no exercise, unsanitary jelly pails), to insufficient food and drink (two slices of bread and two drinks of water per day) (Prison Association of New York, 1916, p. 427). In effect, it was a modern-day Bastille.

In the article, Tannenbaum accused the supervisor of the rock quarry of being a "bully" by refusing to light a fire in order to provide some warmth to the frozen convicts. In fact, being sent to the cooler and then solitary was a relief to Tannenbaum who had spent weeks fighting legions of bedbugs in his old south cell. In addition, Tannenbaum witnessed a beating of a fellow inmate in the cooler by the keeper, who used a wooden police club, in response to an act of verbal defiance. He also knew of two other beatings by keepers against inmates in solitary confinement.

> This is not all. After beating them they turned the fifty-pound pressure hose on them, knocking them unconscious. Then they were dragged into their cells, allowed their one blanket and forced to sleep on the floor covered with six inches of water.
>
> (Tannenbaum, 1915b: 17)

He then described a riot that occurred when the warden elected to punish over 100 prisoners for the loud and boisterous behavior of a few who were celebrating the Fourth of July. This meant no privileges and lockup in their cells. Later, a full-scale riot broke out in the mess hall, with inmates attacking guards and throwing objects (Tannenbaum, 1915c). The riot was put down through the firing of live warning shots from several guards, and the group was escorted into lockup. However, other inmates decided to strike in solidarity against the policies of the warden, which led to the riot in the first place. This resulted in a work stoppage by that part of the reformatory not confined to their cells. Fires soon broke out in the various shops, destroying quite a bit of machinery. Windows were broken as well. Tannenbaum became a spokesperson for the disturbance and was promptly sent to the cooler. After 4 days, the

JAIL: ONE YEAR ON BLACKWELL'S ISLAND

Figure 4.3 Inmates at Blackwell's Island Penitentiary preparing for their breakfast, 1875

inmates were so hungry that many returned to work, and slowly, the institution resumed its normal functioning. "I want to repeat what I once said to him personally [Warden Hayes] that, I would not place him in charge of eighteen hundred dogs, let alone eighteen hundred human beings" (Tannenbaum Collection, Box 2, Folder D, Butler Library, Columbia University, correspondence of 29 June 1915).

Several months after leaving the penitentiary, Frank Tannenbaum returned to Blackwell's Island as a guest of the new corrections commissioner. The institution had changed dramatically. Convicts were allowed to play baseball, join a glee club, read newspapers, talk, and write as many letters as they wished (Tannenbaum, 1916). They were even permitted to decorate their cells and form a league to protect them from unfair disciplinary action. To quote Tannenbaum (1916: 24):

> For the warden, I want to say that he is a clean, capable man, doing the best he can with the situation, anxious to do better whenever possible. It is true that he does not believe in self-government for prisoners as does Thomas Mott Osborne, but then there are not many in the prison world who see as far as Osborne does.

Several well-to-do supporters felt that Frank Tannenbaum's future actually lay in the university and encouraged him to enter Columbia University in the fall of 1916. As we already know, on the day of his release from prison, Frank toured the campus at Morningside as a guest of several friends (*New York Tribune,* March 11, 1915, p. 4). Tannenbaum explicitly acknowledged the help of Mrs. Grace Hatch Childs in the foreword of *Wall Shadows.* Mrs. Childs read of Frank's "eloquence in court" and thereupon asked for an audience with the young Tannenbaum. She not only offered to help Frank financially upon his entrance into Columbia University, but lobbied university officials to permit his matriculation (Box 7, folder C(3), letters of Richard Childs to Tannenbaum, dated Feb 28, 1968 and undated). To quote her husband's letter of May 30, 1974 (Archives, Columbia University Seminars, File Ay6869):

> The first procession of the unemployed [came] to the Church across the street from our home on lower Fifth Avenue . . . and she lingered over Frank's little speech in court—as many others did. Why should she, newly arrived in New York and unschooled in its affairs, send him word as his prison term expired, that she would like to have him come to see her?
>
> So, I came home one afternoon to find him there with her. She had asked how she could help him. His one desire in life was a college education, although he had not had high school preparation! Fred [E. Stagg] Whitin, a prison reformer, arranged it all by the way of special courses and credits, and three professors had to rewrite their courses.

As a result, Professor Carleton Hayes lobbied Columbia University and its dean, Frederick P. Keppel, to permit Frank's entrance, especially since Frank had neither attended high school nor had a diploma (Whitfield, 2013: 100). E. Stagg Whitin, who was prominent in the National Committee on Prison Labor, was a Columbia graduate (1905) and obtained his doctorate in political science from Columbia in 1908 (Hirschhorn, 1997: 10, 12). It is also reported that Thomas Mott Osborne, then warden of Sing Sing Penitentiary, exercised some influence on his admission (Hale, 1995: 221). In fact, both Whitin and Osborne had been members of the New York State Prison Reform Commission in 1913. In a series of letters between the two, Frank sent Grace Childs copies of his grades. She was then the young wife of Richard S. Childs, a prominent New York businessman and municipal reformer.

JAIL: ONE YEAR ON BLACKWELL'S ISLAND

Mrs. Childs, the daughter of a prominent Chicago lawyer, studied social work in New York City and was active for many years in the Charity Organization Society (cf. Tannenbaum Collection, Box 2, Folder C(1); Box 25, Balance of Power Folder, letter from Richard Childs to Frank, dated Feb. 10, 1969, Butler Library, Columbia University).

According to Frank, he entered Columbia on a conditional acceptance because he lacked a high school diploma (Trooboff, 1961: 3).[1] One condition was that he had to maintain a B average "in all his college courses which corresponded in subject to those of the entrance requirement[s]." This conditional acceptance also had a latent political purpose, as illustrated by an event in December 1917.

Early that month, the *New York Times* (December 1, 1917) reported that Frank Tannenbaum was at a public event to form a League of Labor and Political Prisoners, allegedly to help "provide bail and supply legal defense to men and women whose arrest for violation of American laws." The *Times* reporter questioned the efficacy of the organization as merely a front for the IWW resurgence, since there were prominent IWW activists in attendance, as well as anarchist literature. Sensing that he might be in trouble at Columbia, Frank immediately wrote a letter to the editor and made copies available to his professors and Frank D. Fackenthal, official secretary to Columbia College. In his letter, Tannenbaum wrote:

> May I correct the impression given by your report of the meeting which took place at the New Star Casino last night. The meeting was held to raise money for the defence of labor and political prisoners and had no other object. The circular which you print was not distributed by the league and does not represent the object of that organization.
>
> In justice to the men and women arrested for their connection with the I.W.W., I want to state as emphatically as I can that this meeting and the organization which sponsored it has absolutely no connection with the I.W.W.
>
> As for myself, I want to say that I am not averse to fighting for a worthy cause and the cause of the Allies, to my mind, has many of the elements which make it a worthy one.

The *Times* never published Tannenbaum's letter to the editor, but Frank did receive a formal response from Secretary Fackenthal on December 3, 1917: "I must confess, however, that I am sorry that you are taking part in a movement of this kind just now as I feel it is sure to

31

get in trouble sooner or later" (Columbia University Archives, Central File 275, correspondence in folder Ta 1910–1918). It was a warning that Frank's conditional acceptance into Columbia University could be in jeopardy.

He would take a slight detour in his studies to serve in the U.S. Army from August 1918 until February 1919, being honorably discharged from the 20th Division, Fort Dix, New Jersey, at the rank of sergeant (Box 57, Miscellaneous military documents).[2] The experience resulted in Tannenbaum writing two papers on the vocational education of military conscripts and the effect of military life on recruits (Tannenbaum, 1919a). Indeed, he was quite critical of military camp life. Tannenbaum even sent one of these memos to the War Labor Policies Board in Washington, D.C.

Frank became a member of Honors Forum of Columbia College for 1916–1917, *The 1918 Columbian* (New York: Columbia University Press, p. 204). Tannenbaum was also a member of the 1916–1917 Economics Club at Columbia, and again made the Honors Forum for 1917–1918 in *The 1919 Columbian* (New York: Junior Class at Columbia College, p. 139). In June 1920, Tannenbaum was elected to Phi Beta Kappa, according to *The Columbian* (New York: Schilling Press, 1921, p. 249). The same source also lists Frank as the president of the Intercollegiate Socialist Society Chapter (ISC) (*The 1919 Columbian*, p. 202). Of interest, the ISC was founded in 1905 by Upton Sinclair (Dell, 1927: 103; Harris, 1975: 75).

Tannenbaum finished his undergraduate course work at the end of 1920, even though he was also in the U.S. Army for a brief stint before World War I ended. He immediately enrolled in graduate school at Columbia University, intending to major in political science, and completed some coursework up until 1922, when he ceased to be a graduate student.

Frank ultimately received his bachelor's degree in economics and history (highest honors, Phi Beta Kappa) at Columbia University on June 1, 1921. In fact, he was regarded by one of his professors, Dr. Carleton Hayes in history, as "one of the best students we have had in years in Columbia College" (Box 3, Hayes Folder, letter dated Oct. 21, 1918). The *New York Times* (June 5, 1921) wrote an article reporting that Tannenbaum had graduated with honors, but that few in attendance were aware he was a "former radical and agitator" who had served jail time on Blackwell's Island. George Palmer Putnam (1921), founder of the publishing house, G. P. Putnam's Sons, even wrote an article for the

New York Times about Frank's recent college degree at Columbia and his work as a prison reformer and writer. Indeed, Putnam quotes Tannenbaum about his desire for higher education to this effect:

> Because I resented the ridicule of the papers. They said I was only an ignorant boy. In effect, they said, "If he only had an education, he would understand—and act rationally." Then and there I determined no one ever again could call me ignorant of the education of books, no matter what the cost . . . The day I left Blackwell's Island, I started toward Columbia.

Tannenbaum (1921a) actually wrote a response to the coverage of his graduation in the *New York Times,* arguing the higher education was designed to stimulate "originality, of permitting one to choose and pick and grow." Nevertheless, Tannenbaum abandoned his prior fiery rhetoric against capitalism and now extolled the virtues of his college education and that of Columbia University. A political conversion was underway. The Associated Press reported upon his graduation that Tannenbaum had "discarded his radical views and now takes the attitude of a liberal in matters pertaining to economics and psychology" (*Ironwood Daily Globe* (Michigan), "Once a Jail Bird; Now Honor Student," June 4, 1921, p. 1.) There were further reports that he declared he was not an anarchist, socialist, or member of the IWW (*Jeffersonville Star* (Indiana), "Columbia's Gem" June 25, 1921, p. 2).

While a student at Columbia, Frank still kept in touch with several prominent socialist organizations, such as the Rand School of Social Sciences and the Intercollegiate Socialist Society—both based in New York City. Early in his student career, on April 21, 1917, Tannenbaum voiced a personal opinion about the IWW in correspondence to Jerry F. Grant, who was writing a book about the organization. Tannenbaum had this to say about his days as an IWW organizer:

> I have not been so closely associated with the I.W.W. during the last year as I might, so that I am not fully acquainted with the present condition of the organization. But the I.W.W. that I knew I shall always look back upon with the greatest reverence. Nowhere have I found that idealism, that love of one's kind, that social mindedness and sincerity. Nowhere as yet have I seen that willingness to sacrifice, that exulting joy in

human progress, that hope and faith in human progress and a more beautiful life.

The men and women that I knew in the I.W.W., the hard working, rugged and aspiring human beings, whose whole life seemed bound up with the struggles of their class to rise above its poverty and disorganization, were in human worth amongst the best I know.

The I.W.W. is the foreshadowing of a working-class organization that in the fact of current tendencies seems inevitable. The I.W.W. may never fulfill its purpose to organize a mighty industrial democracy, but it is serving the purpose of a pioneer in the struggle for equitable organization of our industrial life and as a pioneer it has suffered the misrepresentation and calumnies usually heaped upon those who foreshadow the better and bigger things in life.

(Box 3, Folder G, Tannenbaum collection)

Some observers argued that Tannenbaum had finally converted to the "Establishment." It was anarchist Alexander Berkman, a colleague of Emma Goldman, who warned Frank about the conservative tendencies of attending Columbia University (Box 2, Folder B1, Berkman letter of May 21, 1915). However, Tannenbaum felt otherwise. Indeed, in a letter to the editor of the *New York Call*, Tannenbaum (1919b) wrote:

The implication in the article was that I have accepted the present economic regime and have become a defender of it. This is simply not true.

My interests in Mr. Osborne's work which are centered about the humanitarian aspect for decency for weak and helpless men behind prison bars, on one hand, and the interesting social experiment which he is carrying on, on the other, have no bearing and have had no influence upon my political and social views. I have not been reformed in the sense that I have abandoned them. Substantially my opinions today are the same as they were in 1914, when I was sentenced to prison. I am just as firmly convinced as I ever was that the whole capitalist system must ultimately go by the board and that a new and better world must and will be built by the workers.

[Tannenbaum, Box 2, Butler Lib., Columbia
University, Folder C(1)]

Nevertheless, Tannenbaum was influenced quite strongly during his undergraduate years by Professor John Dewey, known to have been instrumental in the development of American "pragmatism," Jeffersonian liberalism, and educational reform. Columbia University was also under tremendous political pressure by moneyed elites to purge "radical" faculty during this era. In a December 3, 1917, *New York Times* (p. 11) article titled "Butler Condemns College Bolsheviki," the president of the college promised to fire any university professor with communist leanings, and had already fired several faculty members who displayed an anti-American attitude. Several students had also been expelled from Columbia for opposing the draft and World War I. Tannenbaum was well aware of these political firings and even chaired a student committee to address these issues (Whitfield, 2013: 101). The statutes of Columbia University gave it authority to dismiss a student who engaged in "conduct unbecoming a gentleman" (Box 496, Columbia University Archives, Central Files, Frederick Keppel Folder, Letter to Keppel from President Nicholas Murray Butler, dated March 5, 1917, in folder dated Jan. 1916–June 1922). Frank clearly saw the writing on the wall and tempered his previous radical activities. He would remain in contact with Dewey long after his graduation from Columbia, and pragmatism slowly tempered Frank's early radical views.

By this time, Frank had married the former Esther Abramson on June 1, 1917, in Bronx, New York.[3] Little is known about Miss Abramson, except that she was single and stated her occupation as a stenographer. However, from 1914 to 1918, she worked in a rare book shop in Manhattan where Ms. Abramson handled rare letters, manuscripts, and other documents. She was born in New York City of parents (Soloman and Sarah) who emigrated from Russia. She traveled with Tannenbaum during the summer of 1920 on his car tour of American prisons and accompanied him on several trips to Mexico, beginning in 1922. What is not well known is that a son, Zalkind Tannenbaum, was born to this union on November 4, 1925, in Manhattan, as well as a daughter, Sara Nessa Tannenbaum, also born in Manhattan on June 29, 1927.[4] But Frank Tannenbaum proved to be a poor husband, as he was often absent during the 1920s on various assignments and lectures across North America and in Mexico. In personal letters to his wife, he referred to her as "Zoozoo" and himself as "Puts." At the very time when his wife had given birth to their son, Tannenbaum entered the doctoral program at the Brooking's Institution in Washington, D.C., circa 1925—further separating him from his wife and son. There was clearly some bitterness by his wife that on the birth of his son Frank was in Mexico and only had pictures of him (Box 3, Folder M(1), letter to Frank from R. McGowan, May 18, 1926; Box 5, Folder T(2), telegrams).

Figure 4.4 A photo of Esther Abramson fishing in the 1920s

Figure 4.5 An early 1930's photo of Esther Abramson and her two children, Zalkind and Sara Ness

Notes

1 Records from the Registrar at Columbia University confirm that Frank entered Columbia in September 1916 as a "non-matriculated" student. Communication with Academic Records and Registration, Columbia University, April 29, 2014.
2 Confirmed by National Personnel Records Center, St. Louis, Missouri. Request No. 2–11645244933, dated December 12, 2013.
3 Certificate and Record of Marriage, State of New York, Borough of Bronx, Cert. No. 1992. Municipal Archives, City of New York, New York.
4 From "Births Reported in 1925—Borough of Manhattan," (New York: O'Connell Press); see "Births Reported in 1927—Borough of Manhattan" (New York: O'Connell Press).

5

FRANK'S ASSOCIATION WITH THOMAS MOTT OSBORNE

By this time, Tannenbaum had made contact with progressive prison reformer Thomas Mott Osborne, who was at the time the warden of Sing Sing Penitentiary. Writing to district attorney of Westchester County, Frederick Weeks, Tannenbaum stated (Box 5, Folder W, Letter dated January 15, 1916):

> I first heard of Mr. Osborne and his work while in solitary con-finement in the penitentiary on Blackwell's Island. The news reached me through a friend of Mr. Osborne's who was then investigating city prisons . . . I did not believe in prison reform, my confinement in the penitentiary during a reform administra-tion did not make me very sanguine as to its benefits. I had seen men driven insane as a result of solitary confinement. I had seen others and had myself suffered the tortures of extreme hunger and thirst while wallowing in dirt upon the hard stone floor of the cooler and only a thin blanket for covering.

Tannenbaum then proceeded to list all the differences he noted after several visits to Sing Sing penitentiary at the invitation of Warden Thomas Mott Osborne. In particular, he noted that prison discipline was largely dispensed by the self-government of the convicts. "Their court-room is, I believe, one of the finest self-government educational institu-tions to be found anywhere."

Osborne himself came from a well-to-do background, had graduated from Harvard University, was a former mayor of Auburn, New York, and became interested in prison reform. He was born on September 23, 1859, in Auburn, New York, and the prison there was a dominant and mysterious institution, having been constructed in 1816. In fact, the Osborne family owned the local newspaper called *The Auburn Citizen*. As a young boy,

Figure 5.1 Frank on one of his visits to Sing Sing Penitentiary in 1916, most likely as a guest inmate

Osborne had been taken inside the walls of Auburn Prison, and the experience gave him nightmares (Osborne, 1914; Tannenbaum, 1930a: 7). Subsequently, Osborne became mayor of Auburn and was active in upstate Democratic politics. He represented the anti–Tammany Hall wing of the party. From the very beginning, reports Tannenbaum, Osborne was skeptical of the new-fangled penitentiary, observing that convicts came "out as bad as they came in—or worse." Much of his early experience with corrections came through a farm school for wayward boys and girls called the George Junior Republic, which attempted a form of self-government (Murphy, 2008). Osborne served on the board of this organization for some 15 years, beginning in 1896.

Unlike most prison officials who came up through the ranks and were often political appointees, Osborne was an educated man who read extensively. It was said that he could "run through a Gilbert and Sullivan score" by memory on the piano and that his knowledge of the classics in literature was extraordinary (Chamberlain, 1935: 18; Chapman, 1927a, 1927b). Osborne's interest in prison reform was fueled by reading prison literature, such as Donald Lowrie's (1912) book *My Life in Prison,* McNair's *Prisoners Their Own Warders* (1899), and Cook's *Prisons of the World* (1891). Upon the election of a new governor in 1913, one William Sulfzer, Osborne found himself appointed as chairman of a prison commission of inquiry.

As the newly appointed head of New York state's Commission on Prison Reform, Osborne elected to personally spend 1 week as prisoner Thomas Brown (Prisoner 33333X) in Auburn Penitentiary, circa

Figure 5.2 1916 photo of Frank with Warden Thomas Mott Osborne at Sing Sing Penitentiary

Figure 5.3 October 1913 photo of Thomas Mott Osborne posing as an inmate at Auburn Penitentiary

September 29, 1913.[1] He would later write a book on this experience titled *Within Prison Walls*, as well as another monograph in 1916 on the subject of prison reform. After entering Auburn Penitentiary, Osborne was allowed to address all of the 1,400 inmates, asking them to treat him as a regular prisoner so that he could "break down the barriers between my soul and the souls of my brothers" (Tannenbaum, 1930a: 9). It is reported that although the assembled convicts were initially suspicious, they ultimately applauded Osborne. During his 1-week stay, this strange visitor ate prison slop, carried his own bucket, marched in lock-step, and even served 14 hours in solitary confinement on just bread and water.

When he finished his "indefinite" prison term of 1 week, Osborne again addressed the multitude of convicts in the prison chapel. Stating that he would never forget this experience and never forget the convicts he had met and listened to, the men before him broke out into applause. The response from the press and elite members of the "respectable" community was not as positive. Osborne was labeled a "dilettante" and ill advised. Nevertheless, Chairman Osborne left Auburn Penitentiary with several ideas: chief among them was that most of the prisoners were regular human beings—convicted of criminal behavior, of course—but regular working-class men. This assumption was at variance with established criminological cannons, originating out of Positivism, that the criminal was a pathological, evil deviant (Lombroso, 1911; Healy 1915).

A second idea that emerged from conversations with inmates (not correctional staff) was Osborne's notion that greater freedom within the prison could be used to mold inmate behavior, and that convicts should have some say about discipline within the penitentiary. This was, of course, a Progressive Era–idea and at variance with the principle of "less eligibility," which has historically guided the creation of the penitentiary since the 18th century (Sellin, 1944, 1976; Schwendinger & Schwendinger, 1970).

With the new state governor in power, Osborne lobbied his political masters to appoint a political confidant as the new warden at Auburn Penitentiary. That man's name was Charles Rattigan. Osborne persuaded the new warden of Auburn to allow an election of a prisoners' committee to discuss problems within the penitentiary. A committee of 49 convicts was elected by secret ballot and met with Osborne alone—without the warden or guards present. According to Tannenbaum, a ribald discussion ensued about what a prisoner's committee might do. Ultimately, the group decided to form a "Good Conduct League," which would be entrusted with run-of-the-mill disciplinary problems among inmates, such as violations of prison rules, simple assault including sexual matters, stealing, dope, smuggling, and the like. The warden allowed the league to form, and soon, this inmate committee was actually hearing cases of discipline.

As a result of the league, inmates were released from their cells on Sunday and allowed to attend a Sunday meeting in the chapel, where the program was often music. This was a dramatic change from 100 years of the silent system and the customary weekend lockdown. Friction between the warden and the new league manifested itself in a jurisdictional squabble. Again, Osborne intervened and persuaded the warden to give up disciplinary actions in all but five categories (Tannenbaum, 1930a: 52): assault upon an officer, deadly assault upon another inmate, refusal to work, strike, and attempt to escape. Initially, convicts at Auburn were opposed to assuming disciplinary control, but during a mass meeting in the chapel ultimately voted to accept control.

This shift in disciplinary control had some ancillary effects. Relations between convicts and guards improved. Convicts got access to the exercise yard in large numbers, and contrary to predictions, there were no riots or stabbings.

In the meantime, there had been a scandal at Sing Sing Penitentiary, located on the banks of the Hudson River just north of New York City. The warden was retiring under a cloud of scandal and accusations of graft (Tannenbaum, 1930b). Shortly before in 1913, a grand jury condemned conditions at the penitentiary, first constructed in 1826. After much to and fro, Osborne was persuaded to accept the position, again largely relying on the opinion of convicts he already knew at Auburn and Sing Sing. When Osborne entered this fortress penitentiary in November 1914, Frank Tannenbaum was already in jail at Blackwell's Island, midway through his 1-year sentence. Osborne immediately assembled all 1,496 convicts and announced that he was against the "stool pigeon" system and that heretofore, the inmates would have to step forward and exercise responsibility for the safety of both the guards and themselves. It was a familiar theme, and those members of the dangerous classes gave their new warden a rousing cheer.

Osborne allowed reporters access to Sing Sing, and they reported no fires or strikes by the convicts as the newly installed warden made his rounds. He immediately made efforts to improve prison food and asked the prisoners' committee to form a prison court. The prisoners responded with requests for changes in prison rules, most significantly the formation of a convict court for the adjudication of disciplinary infractions (Tannenbaum, 1930b: 158). Instead of retaining some jurisdiction,

Osborne turned over all prison disciplinary infractions to the new convict court, with the right of appeal to the warden's court if either party was unsatisfied with the outcome. This decision ran against the grain of the entire U.S. prison system, and therefore represented a paradigm shift—as well as a threat to established elite and bureaucratic interests who had created the penitentiary in the early 19th century. As Tannenbaum (1930b: 189) noted, this approach challenged the very basis of criminologic positivism and the prison itself:

> The drab and often horror-filled prisons that were typical up to 1910, their small cells, absolute silence, their inmates with shaven heads and striped clothing; their rule of lockstep, iron chains, cages, iron balls, the dungeon, handcuffs, whipping, aye, even the straight-jacket—all still common at the time that Osborne began his campaign—could only be maintained . . . on the assumption that prisoners were unlike other men.
>
> It was his belief that men in prison could be treated as other men, and that in such treatment lay the possibilities of reconstructing their habits, redirecting their energies, of remodeling their interests, and of reshaping their activities.

This new atmosphere resulted in shop discipline being delegated to inmate representatives rather than prison guards. A prison band was formed, as well as a knitting class to aid the Polish Relief Committee. Tannenbaum was so enthusiastic in his description of Osborne's achievements that he characterized Sing Sing as a "college for the remaking of men" (Tannenbaum, 1930c: 266).

Of course, this was an overly sentimental view. Prison assaults still occurred, but there was a reduction in their number. Escapes were cut down by more than half. The number of men transferred to Dannemora for insanity dropped by 50 percent (Tannenbaum, 1930c: 269). Inmate suicides appeared to have diminished (Field, 1915: 109). Frank documents how the inmates themselves asked to establish a Mutual Welfare League whose primary focus would be education using other prisoners in the role of teachers and supervisors. Over a majority of the Sing Sing population signed up for classes from the new league. The prisoners even established a visitors' bureau, giving guided tours to members of the public. Tannenbaum further describes a fire that broke out in the chapel when it was occupied with 1,000 inmates and how the league's executive officers organized an exit and then marshaled a convict fire brigade to help put out the conflagration.

The goings-on at Sing Sing, dramatic as they were, aroused strong public interest. Osborne was called upon to engage in frequent speaking engagements, the press was allowed access to the penitentiary, and numerous visitors dropped by to see Sing Sing for themselves. However, in the background, there was growing concern: long-vested interests were being threatened. In particular, Osborne replaced the long-standing "spoils" system upon which local business vendors had relied in supplying the penitentiary with food stuffs and other items.

So, for the first year of Osborne's tenure as warden, Tannenbaum (1930c: 270) notes that Sing Sing became a "community" of sorts. A new form of social organization was created to displace, or at least compete with, the historic and pervasive criminal subculture of gangs, professional alliances, and organized crime. On his first anniversary at Sing Sing, the inmates reportedly cheered their warden for some 12 minutes—an event certainly unique in the annals of American corrections, even today.

One of the interesting sanctions of the convict court was, among others, suspension from membership in the Mutual Welfare League. This meant not only confinement in one's cell, but also the denial of privileges and programs sponsored by the league. It also resulted in peer group ostracism by the convicts themselves, not the guards or penal administration (Tannenbaum, 1930c: 303). Although the inmates at Sing Sing still experienced fights, narcotics, sodomy, and even attempted escapes, it was the general consensus—even among the guards—that these problems had been reduced under the new social order within the penitentiary.

Shortly after Tannenbaum's release from Blackwell's Island Penitentiary in March, Osborne appeared at a public meeting at Cooper Union in New York City. There, he agreed with Tannenbaum that conditions at the local penitentiary were unsanitary and, in effect, constituted a form of torture (*New York Times,* April 18, 1915, p. 15, Part II). He also took the unconventional position that inmates should be paid for work "to the rate of wages prevailing outside the prison."

Despite Osborne's bold experiment, there were vested interests who disagreed with his policies. Among them was the head of the New York state prison department, who was a critic of Osborne and kept up a series of critical correspondence with Osborne himself and various news media outlets in the hope that Osborne would resign. It is relevant to note that while a member of the Prison Association of New York in 1913, Osborne and its members actually opposed the nomination of John Riley to become superintendent of prisons on the basis that he had "no positive qualifications for the position" (Minutes of Executive Committee of Prison Association, April 17, 1913, New York City, p. 2). The matter came to a head when the superintendent started interfering with transfers to and from Sing Sing—deliberately ignoring the league and the convict court. This led to a very public dispute between Warden Osborne and the superintendent, and to staff from Albany interviewing convicts who had been transferred by Osborne and might be hostile to him. According to Tannenbaum, Osborne and his staff even caught a state prison agent stealing the warden's confidential papers. Behind the scenes, there was ambivalence from the governor's office, who had appointed Osborne. The new Republican governor, Charles Whitman, had gained office as a successful district attorney whose prosecutions had sent four men to Sing Sing's electric chair (Tannenbaum, 1931a: 378, 381).

The internal campaign by the superintendent of state prisons reached fruition with the publication of an article in the *New York Tribune* on August 5, 1915 (p. 1) titled "Osborne Must Go by Tuesday or Be Ousted." This strategy gained some editorial support across the state, but then petered out. Then, the superintendent started providing information to the local district attorney for Westchester County, New York on especially controversial issues of sexual perversion or homosexuality in prison. He also asked the New York State Commission of Prisons to investigate.

Against the wishes of his colleagues, one of the more conservative commissioners decided to become a self-appointed investigator and brought allegations before the district attorney that Warden Osborne had committed perjury by denying any knowledge of acts of sexual perversion at Sing Sing. The district attorney's grand jury, based on this rather one-sided investigation, indicted some 21 Sing Sing inmates for sexual acts, and indicted Osborne for perjury. Tannenbaum (1933: 243–245) records that the indictment against Osborne resulted in two unusual gatherings at Carnegie Hall in early 1916. About 2 weeks after the Westchester grand jury had indicted Osborne, some 3,500 people packed the famous music hall to defend Warden Osborne and extol his virtues. Even Judge Wadhams, who had sentenced Frank Tannenbaum to Blackwell Island Penitentiary, addressed the crowd in support of Thomas Mott Osborne. The indictment of Osborne created an uproar among church groups, and various newspaper editorials across the state were outraged in their criticism. The district attorney's office was losing the battle for public opinion. Complicating the government's strategy was that none of the indicted inmates, facing upwards of 40 years in penitentiary, offered to testify against Warden Osborne in exchange for leniency and favorable treatment by the superintendent of state prisons.

The matter proceeded to trial, but here, the district attorney was now facing a defendant who was educated, knowledgeable, and had resources to put forward an affirmative defense. Instead of resigning, Osborne took a leave of absence in order to protect his reforms at Sing Sing and prepare for trial. His lead defense attorney was none other than prominent trial lawyer George Gordon Battle, a graduate of the University of North Carolina and Columbia University Law School.

As it happened, many of the witnesses for the district attorney were impeached or shown to be biased. Several of the state's witnesses even gave sworn statements to the defense that they had been cajoled into giving evidence on promise of favors and lenient treatment. Finally, it was revealed that the state prison commissioner who made the allegations of perjury had "no authority to administer a valid oath" to Warden Osborne (Tannenbaum, 1931b: 616). On a motion to dismiss, the judge quashed the charge against Osborne. Later, with the case in shambles, the new district attorney dismissed all the remaining cases against the inmates, as well as other charges against Osborne. On his triumphant return to Sing Sing, the inmates, staff, and the executive of the Mutual Welfare League gave Warden Osborne a banner celebration, which included renditions from the prison band.

Nevertheless, within 2 months, the newly appointed superintendent of prisons began to undermine Warden Osborne by issuing orders from Albany without even consulting Osborne first. One of those orders was that long-term inmates with good conduct records could not be allowed to work outside the walls of Sing Sing. This had been a historic practice, particularly among the "lifers." Osborne refused to comply, and instead submitted his resignation.

While warden of Sing Sing, Osborne invited Tannenbaum to visit the penitentiary as early as March 20, 1915, soon after Frank's own release from Blackwell's Island (*New York Tribune,* March 21, 1915, p. 6). Osborne had followed Frank's articles in *The Masses*, and later arranged for Tannenbaum to spend a short stay as an anonymous prisoner in the fall of 1916. By 1917, however, Osborne had been deposed from his position at Sing Sing, and had taken over as superintendent of the U.S. Naval Prison located in Portsmouth, New Hampshire. He had secured this position through the help of Franklin Delano Roosevelt, who was then under secretary of the Navy. Indeed, it was Osborne who first forwarded Tannenbaum's (1920) article on prisons to the editor of *The*

Atlantic Monthly, who agreed to publish it. Osborne would also underwrite Tannenbaum's tour of southern prisons in 1922 (Box 4, Osborne Folder, Tannenbaum collection). Toward his death in October 1926, Osborne was working on a book of his experiences as warden of Sing Sing, titled *Politics and Prisons*, which was never published. In fact, Osborne had also written a report on the U.S. Naval Prison in Portsmouth, which was never made public (Box 4, Osborne Folder, letter of October 8, 1917).

In a sentimental letter to Tannenbaum, Osborne wrote: "You know one of the Auburn lads once explained my possession of the prisoners' confidence by saying that the boys looked upon me 'as at least half a crook'" (Box 4, Osborne Correspondence, Letter to Tannenbaum by Osborne, dated November 3, 1919). Both Osborne and Tannenbaum kept in touch even after Osborne left his position as warden at the Portsmouth Naval Prison, circa 1920. As for Osborne's view of most prison experts and social workers, he had this to say: "They just come together every year [for a conference], tear around to a lot of meetings, do a lot of talking about unessentials, listen to papers from dreary and hopelessly well-meaning mediocrities, and disperse" (Box 4, Osborne folder, letter dated May 14, 1923). His view of the American Prison Association was equally blunt: "The American Prison Association is nothing but camouflage for the wardens' association, bound to sustain the old system" (Box 4, Osborne folder, correspondence of April 17, 1923). Osborne's views of the traditional voluntary organizations, such as the New York Prison Association and the Howard League, was "that they have their roots too deep in the old system and they can't change. They must be discarded and superseded" (Box 4, Osborne Folder, Ibid.). After Osborne left his appointment at the U.S. Naval Prison in 1920, he was considered for appointment as warden to at least eight other prisons—each time losing the assignment to others (Box 4, Osborne folder, letter of Dec. 18, 1925 to Tannenbaum). He became a consultant to the governor of Colorado, recommending that the current warden be fired, only to discover that civil service rules prevented his firing without a full evidentiary hearing. After this experience, Osborne would observe in frustration:

> Here is a concrete example of how our stupid and corrupt politics will block all attempts to bring about better conditions in the prisons. And meanwhile the amount of crime is appalling and the public vibrates between stolid indifference and angry cries for vengeance against some particularly brutal criminal,

who is too frequently a product of the very correctional institutions themselves. So we continue, chasing around the vicious circle.

(Osborne Papers, Box 271, National Society
of Penal Information folder, 1924)

In 1924, however, Osborne encouraged Tannenbaum to write a book about the prison problem and the impact of Osborne's Mutual Welfare League. In correspondence to Ama Morris, dated May 8, 1924, Osborne had this to say about Frank's book project:

He will begin with the boy, lured into lawlessness by mere mischief, or the influence of the gang, or a Fagin; sent to a reform school; coming out after his natural instincts have long repressed, with a knowledge of vice and finding his old better comrades gone ahead—leaving him no recourse but gang and the criminal.

[Box 3, Folder M(2), letter of June 18, 1930
from Ama Morris to Tannenbaum]

Indeed, Frank's book, published some 14 years later and titled *Crime and the Community*, was heavily influenced by his contact with the late Thomas Mott Osborne (Barnes, 1926). But first, Tannenbaum would finish a monograph about Osborne himself, titled *Osborne of Sing Sing* (1933).

Osborne died while walking home on October 20, 1926. It remains part of the lexicon of American corrections that his body was allowed to lie in state at Auburn Penitentiary, where some 1,400 convicts, in rows of two, solemnly paid tribute to the prison reformer. As the years ebbed by, the state prison administration slowly undermined the Mutual Welfare League at both Auburn and Sing Sing (Barnes, 1926: 358). Historian David Rothman (1980: 131–132), in his assessment of Osborne, concluded that the concept "of a Mutual Welfare League made little impact on prison systems" in the United States. This was because prison wardens and superintendents were loath to give up their disciplinary power to deviant criminals who were in their custody (McLennan, 2008: 443–449). As further noted by Lawrence Friedman (1993: 311), 'the status quo soon reasserted itself. The underlying problem of prisons, of course, was political and social: the men and women locked up were the lumpenproletariat." One might also add that Osborne's approach to prison administration undermined both the principle of "less eligibility," upon which prisons have historically been based, and ran contrary to prevailing notions of criminological positivism (the pathologic medical model of deviance).

After Osborne's death, Frank was able to secure a small stipend from the Social Science Research Counsel to help write the Osborne biography, starting in 1927 (Box 2, Folder A, Letter by Tannenbaum dated November 5, 1927). Tannenbaum's sponsor, the wealthy philanthropist George Foster Peabody, had also contributed the sum of $500 to the project (Box 4, Peabody folder, letter of April 14, 1927). In a letter outlining the project, Tannenbaum stated that he possessed some 40,000 documents from the Osborne estate to underscore the impact of Osborne's work as a prison reformer in the penitentiaries located in Auburn, Sing Sing, and the Portsmouth naval prison. Second, these documents would illustrate the nature of confinement from the prisoners' point of view, including family relations and the "difficulties of adjustment to the community after release" (Box 2, Folder D, letter of September 30, 1927, to Dr. E. Divine, George Washington University). Finally, Tannenbaum saw this voluminous material as providing the basis for an examination of the psychology of the professional criminal.

At the time, the Osborne estate possessed nearly 40,000 letters from convicts sent to Thomas Mott Osborne. This included about 1,000 completed questionnaires by convicts at Auburn and Sing Sing penitentiaries as well.[2] This project, however, never came to fruition. One of the critiques was that the material was over 20 years old, and although undoubtedly correct about the horrendous state of juvenile reform schools, the situation had likely changed (Letter of January 3, 1928, from Prof. George W. Kirchwey, New York School of Social Work, Tannenbaum collection, Box 3, Folders K&L). Frank nevertheless felt the letters were a valuable "contribution to a picture of internal workings of American penal institutions in the early part of the century" (Box 3, Folders K&L, letter to George Kirchway, January 9, 1928). Despite this, Tannenbaum abandoned this book project, but managed to incorporate a small portion of this material into his planned biography of Osborne.

The original manuscript had been titled *The Ordeal of Thomas Mott Osborne* (Tannenbaum Collection, Box 2, Folder E, Letter of March 2, 1932). That work would later be published as *Osborne of Sing Sing* in 1933. Devotees of criminological history will be interested to know that Edwin H. Sutherland, then at the University of Chicago's Department of Sociology in 1931, actually reviewed the Osborne manuscript

(Tannenbaum collection, Box 4, Folder S(1), Letter from Sutherland dated November 14, 1931). Sutherland would observe,

> I do not agree that there is a contrast between Osborne's institutions and all other institutions and that all others were entirely black and his entirely white. I do not for a moment think that you would make a statement to that effect. But it has that effect when you present the first three or four chapters as contrast to Auburn under Osborne.

Feisty as usual, Tannenbaum would reply that it was unlikely he would "undertake a comprehensive change in the organization of the book." He then went on to defend the portrait of the American prison system as he knew it around 1910, stating that, for the most part, they were repressive regimes that depended on torture and inhumane conditions:

> You may recall that in Chapter X of my manuscript entitled "Prison Democracy," I pointed out that all of the disciplinary difficulties from sodomy to crooked letters manifested themselves under the Osborne system, but the method of handling those problems had been completely changed.
> (Letter of November 24, 1931 to E. H. Sutherland,
> Box 4, Folder S(1), Tannenbaum collection)

Ultimately, however, Sutherland replied that he would endorse the book as "an important contribution" to the University of Chicago Press. Of significance, Sutherland took the position that "[m]y hypothesis is that prisons are hopeless and nothing can make them decent. Yours seems to be that a method and personality like Osborne's can reform them" (Tannenbaum Collection, Box 4, Folder S(2), Letter from Sutherland to Tannenbaum, dated December 9, 1931).

Frank would successfully lobby then New York governor, Franklin Delano Roosevelt, to write an introduction to the book as early as 1930. As previously noted, Roosevelt had been a close friend of Osborne, and had authorized an experiment in convict democracy at the naval prison facility in Portsmouth, New Hampshire, while Roosevelt was under secretary of the Navy (Box 1, Correspondence with F.D.R., dated May 12, 1930, and reply, dated May 21, 1930). In lobbying his long-time publisher, G. P. Putnam's Sons, with respect to the Osborne book, Tannenbaum felt it would become a bestseller, writing to the publisher,

"If I don't write you a best seller for this, you ought to dump me in the East River" (Tannenbaum Collection, Box 4, Putnam Folder, Letter of July 19, 1928 to G. P. Putnam). Putnam was not so convinced and declined to publish the completed manuscript in 1930. In fact, Tannenbaum had difficulty finding a publisher for the Osborne book and solicited the help of Alice Brandeis, the wife of Supreme Court Justice Louis Brandeis, to find a publisher (Box 1, Correspondence, June 26, 1932).

At one juncture, Frank even asked if the Osborne estate would purchase 1,000 copies of his book on Thomas Mott Osborne as a means of financing a print run (Box 4, Folder N&O, letter to Charles Osborne dated March 2, 1932). He even thought the book could be published serially in *The Saturday Evening Post*, or as a book of the month. Sadly, G. P. Putnam's Sons rejected the book, suggesting that it would only appeal to a small "group of readers who know something about prison affairs" (Box 4, George Putnam Folder, correspondence dated May 29, 1930). Eventually, the University of North Carolina Press came to the rescue and published *Osborne of Sing Sing* in 1933. Various reviews were positive, but the book never became a publishing success (Feld, 1934; Cantor, 1934; Potter, 1934).

Tannenbaum's book on the late Thomas Mott Osborne was a valiant attempt to accomplish two goals: first, to review the state of prisons in the first third of the 20th century, especially the psychology of imprisonment and release from a convict perspective; second, a biography of Osborne as a prison reformer and how the "old system" schemed to devalue and undermine his achievements in corrections.

The first four chapters of *Osborne of Sing Sing* are organized under the rubric of "The Penal System." Tannenbaum described the typical American prison as a multi-tiered fortress of cell blocks that had changed little from its inception in the early 19th century. Instead of relying on official government discourse, Tannenbaum elected to quote his own experience and publications, including the letters that convicts wrote to Osborne and Tannenbaum's own work for the Wickersham Commission, *Penal Institutions,* Report No. 9 (1931). Tannenbaum (1933: 7) wrote:

> The cell block, with its thousand cells and more, such as we have just depicted, having stood a hundred years without sufficient air and sunshine, without plumbing, damp, insufficiently painted, saturated with the grime and sweat of unwashed human beings who spend more than half of their living time in a space that is barely larger than a good sized dog kennel, cannot be

kept clean—at least cleanliness has been but rarely achieved and that only in the very newest prisons.

Prisoner correspondence described the filth, dirty blankets, vermin, substandard dishware, food infected with weevils and worms, and numerous health problems, including tuberculosis and syphilis. Whether or not these conditions were known to the public, they were clearly known by penitentiary administrators, who threatened punishment (the dark hole or being hung in shackles for 10 hours) to any convict who wished to inform inspectors. As for political elites, these conditions were generally ignored, except when a riot or mass escape brought the attention of liberal reformers, newspaper reporters, and the occasionally well-meaning politician.

Tannenbaum's chapter on prison discipline revealed the use of a regulatory system to inflict further punishment upon inmates, including screen cells, dungeons, chains, whipping (the lash), starvation (bread and water), the use of high-powered water hoses, hand-cuffed to cells, and the like. Frank (1933: 13) correctly characterized these means of discipline as a form of state-sanctioned torture. These were the conditions that Osborne faced "when he challenged the whole scheme of contemporary penal administration," starting in 1910 (p. 29). Importantly, Tannenbaum argued that even with the demise of the "silent system," various methods of torture were still being used across the country.

The next two chapters on the influence of the prison on convicts and their experiences released to the community are still relevant even to contemporary corrections. In these few pages, Tannenbaum let convicts speak from their own letters to Warden Osborne. But first, he quoted from an unpublished manuscript by Osborne. In that manuscript, Osborne noted that many of his predecessors at Sing Sing Penitentiary had been political appointees, who generally lasted no more than 2 years in the position and often resigned under a cloud of corruption, graft, or malfeasance in office (pp. 30–31). The deputy wardens and chief jail keepers, who had risen from the ranks of prison guards, actually ran the prisons and to keep the "lid down," used the "rat" system whereby certain convicts became government "stool pigeons" and received special favors for keeping the general population under surveillance (p. 33). This system, however, ran counter to efforts to habilitate convicts, since it instilled in everyone a sense of distrust of officialdom and of other inmates. Of course, a good deal of contraband smuggling was actually the work of corrupt guards and prison officials.

The prison had an isolating effect—by design and implementation. Prisoners frequently complained that mail was censored or never delivered and that visits were infrequent or disallowed, depending on their disciplinary status. As a result of spending so much time in a small, dank cell, convicts spent their erstwhile hours recalling their own criminal pursuits—both successes and failures. "I . . . felt a certain measure of pride in the knowledge that all of my fellow prisoners believed as I did 'that some day some one was going to pay'" (p. 40).

> Every sound, every face, every movement, is subject to suspicion. The guards watch the prisoners and the prisoners watch the guards. The prisoners watch each other and the warden watches them all. Everyone is suspicious of everyone else. The warden employs prisoners to watch the prisoners and even employs "stool pigeons," "rats," to watch the guards. The atmosphere becomes increasingly surcharged with feeling and fear and hate.
>
> (p. 41)

Tannenbaum, recalling his own jailing and the experience it gave him talking with other convicts, concluded that this atmosphere forced "the prisoner to find his pleasure in living over his past experiences in imagination and in projecting his past pleasures and interests into the future. It lays the foundation for a continued criminal career" (p. 43). He further stated, "Seeing all this crookedness going on around me, after being sent to prison to reform, you can see for yourself, why so many men came back after being sent out" (p. 44).

On the convict's release after serving his sentence, this return is often painful and "doomed to failure." Inmates, particularly those having served many years in the penitentiary, find their support system in shambles: no friends, no home, no money, no job. Inmates are released with bus money and a set of prison-issued clothing. Most return to the community where their previous crime was known and immediately attract the suspicions of local policing agencies. They experience social ostracism and great difficulty securing employment given their criminal records. Many are in ill health due to their imprisonment and cannot hold down legitimate employment for any lengthy period of time. To quote one convict's letter (p. 49):

> I had to get out of my sister's house because they were afraid to get my sickness. I am living in a two dollar furnish room, me & my wife. Its pretty tough. I am too weak to get a job my poor

wife went to work for $4.50 a week. I am nearly crazy & I don't know what to do. The most of the time we don't have enough to eat. I wish that God would kill me so it would be all over.

The denial of legitimate work in the community came face to face with the convict's old lifestyle. "Obstacles and barriers have been thrown across my path until I become discouraged and longed for the old Devil-may-care-life, excitement, fighting, roughness, and money" (pp. 53–54). To Tannenbaum, who had reviewed Osborne's (1914) first book when he worked as a writer for *The Masses*, the warden was one of those rare individuals who "was conscious of the brutalizing effects of the ordinary prison and of the barriers a prison sentence is in any attempt to find a place for an honest livelihood" (Tannenbaum, 1916; 1933: 55).

The remainder of the chapters comprised a biography of Osborne, championing the effects of his penal reforms at Auburn, Sing Sing, and the Portsmouth naval facility. Tannenbaum explained the origins and development of the prisoner-run Mutual Welfare League and how convicts created their own court system to address disciplinary infractions within the prisons. The development of the league also led to the creation of numerous convict committees, and in particular, a push by convicts themselves to develop educational, cultural, and craft programs to keep the prison population occupied with so-called positive pursuits.

The last few chapters detailed how various state elites, including the then-governor of New York and his superintendent of state prisons, conspired to "frame" Osborne for the crime of perjury and managed to secure an indictment from the local county grand jury. Osborne was ultimately exonerated of all charges and later resigned from Sing Sing in 1917, protesting interference from the new superintendent of state prisons who was intent upon thwarting Osborne's reforms. Osborne would spend the next 3 years as warden of the U.S. Naval Penitentiary at Portsmouth, where he dismantled the old penal regime and instituted his reforms. These reforms resulted in strident opposition from mid-level officers who had previously run the prison and fervently believed in the old notions of strict discipline and punishment. Osborne would resign his commission at Portsmouth in 1920. He continued to write and lecture, but was effectively "blackballed" by the traditional prison establishment. In many ways, Osborne's own experiences would be repeated by the work of penologist Thomas Murton. Murton was appointed warden of two Arkansas state prison farms in 1968 and unearthed widespread corruption and numerous graves of convicts who had been murdered when they refused to succumb to the extortion demands from guards and convict trustees appointed by the prison administration (Murton & Hyams, 1969; Murton, 1976). For this effort, Murton was dismissed by the governor and literally run out of the state by threat of prosecution (for grave robbing).

Later, in 1940, Metro-Goldwyn-Mayer pictures attempted to purchase the title to Frank's book on Osborne so that a quasi-fictional motion picture of his life could be produced. This effort never came to fruition because Tannenbaum objected to a movie based on "a purely fictionalized story which has no connection with Osborne and has no bearing on his influence on America prison life" (Box 12, University of North Carolina Folder, letter to W. T. Couch dated March 27, 1940).

It is not well known, however, that Osborne secured funding from relatives and friends, and produced his own movie on prisons released commercially in 1920 during the silent era. In 1919, he had obtained permission to film inside the Portsmouth naval prison and used convicts dressed in old prison stripes as extras in the film. The film was never a commercial success, in part due to the difficulty in distributing it to cinemas, as well as its overt propaganda themes of prison torture—including a death penalty electrocution—and hope for prison reform in the form of the Mutual Welfare League. The film was re-released in 1921 under the title *The Right Way*, and in 1926 titled *Within Prison Walls*.

Notes

1   In the Tannenbaum collection (Box 57), there is a file with Thomas Mott Osborne's actual prison admission records to Auburn, including his prison photo (he was 54 at the time), measurements, and the like. As a fiction, Osborne was committed for the crimes of ignorance and indifference, and given an indefinite life term. Mr. Osborne likely gave this material to Tannenbaum as a gift. See also Box 42, Misc. clippings file for photo of Osborne as inmate Tom Brown at Auburn Penitentiary. Notations on picture circa April 1924.
2   I was unable to find either the 40,000 convict letters or the 1,000 questionnaires in the Osborne papers held at Syracuse University.

6

PRISON WORK, PRISON REFORM, PRISON LABOR

Tannenbaum would keep up his interests in prison reform even while an undergraduate at Columbia University. In 1917, he testified before the New York State Prison Commission on conditions at Clinton Penitentiary in upstate New York, revealing various inhumane and brutal conditions (Leary, 1917). In fact, in a letter to the editor of the *Atlantic Monthly*, Tannenbaum wrote (Box 4, Folder S(1), letter of Jan. 10, 1920 to Mr. Sedgwick):

> The publicity given to prison reform has produced a popular impression that our prison system throughout the country has undergone very important changes. This it seems to me, is, to say the least not quite true. I am not denying that a change for the better has taken place in some of the prisons. Unfortunately, however, that change is rather isolated and exceptional.
>
> I also read it [a paper] [at] a meeting of Sociologists and Psychologists in New York City . . . [T]he discussion did not question the main point in the article—that isolation leads to cruelty and the cruelty phenomena is universal where isolation is the basis of operation on the part of the prison machine.

Two years later in 1921, Tannenbaum published *The Labor Movement: Its Conservative Functions and Social Consequences.* Here, he called for the reorganization of a capitalist market society under a form of government dictated by industrial labor groups pursuing a consensus of community interests.

> The imperialism and militarism of capitalism is opposed by the pacifism and anti-militarism which is general among workers. The trust is met by the industrial union, the competitive by the

cooperative principle, the propaganda of the class in power by the derision and refusal to believe on the part of those whom they would persuade.

(p. 79)

[T]he future government will probably be one composed of representatives of organic groups of industrial workers.

(p. 197)

[T]his change in community organization postulates the elimination of the competitive commercial system, that it assumes the substitution of service for profit in industrial activity; it also takes for granted that production will be for the consumer's interest rather than for the producer's gain.

(p. 197)

In a letter to Eugene V. Debs, who was incarcerated at the Atlanta federal penitentiary under a conviction for inciting sedition, Tannenbaum described unions as a "great revolutionary factor in the community" (Box 1, Correspondence to Debs, June 18, 1921). Debs, of course, was one of the founders of the Industrial Workers of the World (IWW) and a major American socialist leader (Brommel, 1978). Nevertheless, Tannenbaum also argued the inverse—that labor unions were also conservative to the extent they functioned to stabilize society by eliminating individual strife (*Current Opinion,* 1921).

A year earlier, Tannenbaum (1920) had been asked to edit the work of Lord Leverhulme (William H. Lever), a member of the British aristocracy, who favored the 6-hour day but was quite hostile to socialism, anarchism, and Bolshevism. The invitation came from his economics professor, Henry R. Seager at Columbia University, who had an interest in labor and social insurance reform. Lord Leverhulme started the soap and cleaning firm Lever Brothers, earned a fortune through monopolies, and favored British imperialism. Nevertheless, this project was consistent with Frank's own rural upbringing and his penchant for local union activism over central statist institutions. But it also signaled a growing conservatism in Tannenbaum's view of the world.

As a further illustration of his legendary industry, Frank wrote a series—three to be exact—of articles in *The Atlantic Monthly* on the subject of prisons, something he knew well.

The first article, titled "Prison Cruelty," was published in 1920 as Tannenbaum was finishing his undergraduate degree at Columbia University.

His mentor, Thomas Mott Osborne, helped Tannenbaum with a referral to the editors of *The Atlantic Monthly*, who agreed to publish these articles. In this first article, Tannenbaum observed that "cruelty has always marked prison administration. We have records of brutality in prisons stretching over all written history, and including practically every nation of which we have written records" (p. 433). Sub-rosa, prisons inflict cruelty because of the popular assumptions we make about criminals. Here, Tannenbaum borrows from the positivist school in criminology to conclude that to the ordinary person, the criminal "is thus bad, unsocial, a violator of law, and a sinner as well" (p. 435). The primary function of prison, according to Tannenbaum, is to keep the convicts confined. The warden's mission is primarily that of a jailer.

At Blackwell's Island, Tannenbaum delved into the personal to indicate that convicts were not allowed to have pencils or paper or thread in their cells so as to reduce the potential threat of communication (and therefore escape). Isolation cells were used for many disciplinary infractions, and the Auburn silent system was still in vogue, although it was under attack by various prison reformers. This led to the constant violation of prison regulations and a preoccupation with disciplinary infractions by the keepers.

> The greater the number of violations, the more brutal the punishments; for variety of the punishments and their intensification become, in the mind of the warden, the sole means of achieving the intimidation of the prisoner by which he rules.
>
> (p. 438)

Over time, variations in brutality came to include the use of the dark cell, starvation for days at a time, beatings, straitjacketing, handcuffing, hanging to a door, or lifting from the floor. Invoking social psychology, Tannenbaum contended that this prison cruelty was facilitated by notions of difference between the convicts and their keepers.

> This distinction in the mind of the keeper is absolutely essential. It is essential because we cannot brutally impose our will upon our equals and betters. We can do it only to those whom we *believe* to be inferior—different,—and not as good as ourselves.
>
> (p. 439)

Convicts, according to Tannenbaum, reject this notion of inferiority and simply believe that what distinguishes them from the "average Joe" in the community is that they have "been caught and the rest are still to be caught" (p. 440). This notion comes from the published work of Thomas Mott Osborne (1916), who went to great lengths to ridicule the work of most contemporary penologists, especially Cesare Lombroso (1911) Gina Lombroso-Ferrero (1911), and Havelock Ellis (1910). Important to Tannenbaum was the notion that isolation in prison "works in a vicious circle leading on to greater isolation and to more cruelty and more isolation" (1920: 444). The reverse phenomenon of greater social cohesion among convicts through Osborne's program for prisoners' self-government reduces pressures in prison life that give rise to prison cruelty.

A year before the publication of *Wall Shadows*, Tannenbaum (1921b) published a lengthy article in *The Atlantic Monthly* titled "Prison Facts." He starts the article by talking about a conversation he had with a prison warden, whom he described as a man of little formal education except from what he had learned working his way up from a prison guard. "These men can only be treated in one way—that is, strict and steady discipline. Always be just to the men, but punish them quick and sharp when they break the rules" (p. 577). Tannenbaum and his wife were visiting this relatively modern "Auburn type" prison in the western United States, and since it was Sunday, were invited to participate in Sunday chapel services. Tannenbaum then describes a 15-minute service, which was pronounced for the way the inmates shuffled into the church, single file, their heads bowed, shoulders stooping. "There was a listless weariness about these spiritless men, a kind of hopeless resignation, an acceptance of an unrelenting fate and a broken submission" (p. 578). With his wife in tears, Tannenbaum commented that this memory haunted him. "Never before had I seen anything quite so humiliating, inhuman, and sterile" (p. 579). This picture of spiritual stagnation was typical of prisons Tannenbaum had seen.

> There is no spiritual life in the average American prison. There is no hope, no inspiration, no stimulus, no compulsion of the soul to better things. It is hard, cold, frozen, dead.
>
> (p. 580)

Tannenbaum had been on a tour of some 70 prisons during the summer of 1920. He was working that summer for the National Committee on Prisons and Prison Labor, headquartered in New York City, chaired by none other than Thomas Mott Osborne (Tannenbaum Collection, Box 5, Folder T(1)). One of the reasons for the trip was to generate interest in prisoner self-government among American prison wardens.

Tannenbaum recounts how one warden accused him of being someone from "one of them damned reform committees who believe in coddling the prisoners." In this warden's view, he treated the convicts fairly, but woe to the prisoner who is "going to rough-house it." The method of fixing this lapse in discipline was to strap the prisoner over a barrel and "cane him." After that, a 70-pound ball was chained to his ankle and he was returned to the shop from where he caused the trouble.

Various forms of corporal discipline were in vogue at this time, including flogging, straitjackets, the lockstep, bread and water, the dark cell, the iron cage, the underground cell, and extended solitary confinement. However, pressure from outside groups, often disciples of the Progressive Era, was causing prison administrators to gradually ameliorate these punishments. In fact, Tannenbaum searched in vain for the "model" prison—unique, exceptional, a pride to that state. Not surprisingly, he never found such an institution. Indeed, when asked by a newspaperman, "And what did you find?" Tannenbaum responded: "That most of the talk about better days and more intelligent management is all bunk, got up for outside consumption" (T. M. Osborne Papers, Box 268, Misc. clippings, 1900–1923, n.d. article by I. K. Russell).

He also talked about the issue of prison labor, finding that a great percentage of men were functionally idle. These convicts either sat in their cells during the day or occupied an "idle-house" in which they all sat facing one way while under guard. Very few of the prisons paid convicts for their labor, to which Tannenbaum inquired: "And yet, it is asked why the men are not interested and ambitious" (p. 588).

Tannenbaum further described the cells, stating that most prisons at that time were built on the "Auburn" model. This consisted of large walls on the exterior and a multistory cellblock inside where cells were apportioned on tiers or ranges. "A cell is not larger than a good-sized grave stood on end" (p. 586). In the older systems, buckets were used for toilets, and ventilation was poor, even nonexistent. Tannenbaum then describes his own imprisonment on Blackwell's Island in 1914.

> In my own case—and this is typical of the old prison—the old cellblock in Blackwell's Island was bug-ridden. In my day, there were thousands of bugs in my cell. I struggled valiantly, constantly, and industriously. But it was a hopeless fight. I had some books, and the bugs made nests in them. They crept over me when I slept—they made life miserable.
>
> (p. 587)

PRISON WORK, PRISON REFORM, PRISON LABOR

The blankets on the cot in Tannenbaum's cell were "dirty," which was a common occurrence for inmates.

Likewise, most of the prisons surveyed made no serious attempt to educate their convicts. The same was true for health concerns. In concluding his observations of these 70 prisons, Tannenbaum observed:

> There is not a prison in the country, in so far as I have seen them, that does not fall into this general picture in one or more of its phases . . . The present prison system is bad. I have hardly described all its evils. Some cannot be written about without greater finesse and literary subtlety than I possess. Others were hidden from me.
>
> (p. 588)

And although Frank Tannenbaum held out some hope with respect to reforms, mentioning parole, education, self-government, and farm labor, he was not optimistic. Writing in 1921, "all of these are negligible and limited" (p. 588). If we consult some of the early convict literature about the prison, this picture was typical (Lowrie, 1912; Jennings, 1921; Nelson, 1933). All of which leads to the question why Tannenbaum never contextualized the function of the prisons he had surveyed in American society. He offered no overarching theoretical explanation as to why this pattern dominated the nation, other than misguided, unimaginative, and backward wardens and politicians. Coming from a self-admitted syndicalist, this was indeed a contradiction.[1]

The following year, Tannenbaum (1922a) published another article in *The Atlantic Monthly* titled "Facing the Prison Problem." Here, Tannenbaum concluded that the prison was a failure, but insisted that properly conceived, it "should be a healing ground for both the spirit and the body, where the unsocial should be socialized, the weak strengthened, the ignorant educated, the thwarted made to grow (p. 207)." Tannenbaum called for the abandonment of the old cellblock-style penitentiaries and instead favored prison farms, road crews, and supervision outside the dank walls of the modern American prison.

> A large tract of land, a big farm, small barracks, plenty of sunshine and air, and the money for education and for health, for the building of character—these are substitutes for the raising of useless and perverting stone and iron cages.
>
> (p. 211)

He lamented that most wardens were incompetent, and recommended a center where prison officials could be properly trained. Indeed, Tannenbaum doubted that any kind of penal agency was preferable, suggesting that the "function of the state should be, not to punish, but to educate. The place of the penal department ought to be taken by a new bureau, dedicated to health, education, and industry—entrusted to experts in these respective fields" (p. 211). In this regard, Tannenbaum supported the proper classification of prisoners, which was then becoming popular among liberal prison reformers. He called for appropriate medical screening and care of inmates by a physician who was not "a tool of the warden" (p. 212).

On the question of work within prisons, Tannenbaum considered most prison labor essentially slave labor produced under a regime of fear and loathing. Instead, he advocated training that could be transferred to the outside community and commensurate wages to give the convicts "some basis for zest and interest, for ambition and motive" (p. 213). Admittedly, this would require "freedom from the politician," a relationship for which neither Tannenbaum nor others had a feasible solution, since it was the state that financed the building of prisons and wished to run them as cheaply as possible.

Finally, Tannenbaum called for the introduction of the indeterminate sentence so that convicts could be released "when [they are] fit to return to society" (p. 216) Thus, parole should be expanded, concluding that at least half of most penitentiary populations could be released on parole "without proportionately endangering the safety of the community" (p. 216) Invoking the wisdom of his mentor, Thomas Mott Osborne (1914, 1916), Tannenbaum strongly endorsed the creation of prisoner welfare leagues within the confines of the penitentiary, where convicts were given a great deal of authority over their own affairs, including the all-important question of penal discipline. After the publication of *Wall Shadows*, Tannenbaum sought and obtained for his book the endorsement of Eugene V. Debs, then incarcerated in a federal penitentiary (Box 1, Tannenbaum Collection, Correspondence of April 12, 1922, with Theodore Debs). Indeed, the book itself became "one of the most popular reform tracts of the [Progressive] period (Rothman, 1980: 121).

Published in 1922 with a foreword by Thomas Mott Osborne, *Wall Shadows* represented an insider's view of the American prison system rather than an academic treatment. As noted previously, it was based on Tannenbaum's own experiences at Blackwell's Island Penitentiary, as well as his 1920 tour of some 70 prisons across the country.

Tannenbaum (1922b: 5) begins with a historical observation that most readers may have assumed but did not wish to hear: "cruelty has always marked prison administration . . . We have records of brutality in prisons stretching over all written history, and including practically every nation of which we have written records. Prison brutality is both continuous and universal."

In this context, he makes a very important observation about the overall purpose of the penitentiary, whether it be maximum or minimum security.

> The function of the prison is to keep the men confined. The function of the warden is to make sure that the purpose of the prison is fulfilled. He is primarily a jailer . . . He is a jailer first; a reformer, a guardian, a disciplinarian, or anything else, second.
> (Tannenbaum, 1922b: 11–12)

To this end,

> Men in prison are always counted. They are counted morning, noon, and night. They are counted when they rise, when they eat, when they work, and when they sleep. Like a miser hovering over his jingling coins, the warden and the keepers are constantly on edge about the safety of their charges—a safety of numbers first, of well-being afterwards.

As a backdrop for managing large numbers of convicts with a minimum of labor, prison administrators rely upon a host of disciplinary rules to keep prisoners compliant, prevent escapes, and reduce the ever-present threat of riots. To Tannenbaum, this meant a circular relationship between the number of rules and the number of violations. Because prisoners already have their liberty and most of their property taken away, the use of brutality "becomes a matter of administrative procedure and a normal expectation on the part of the prisoner" (Tannenbaum, 1922b: 21). What remains is a method of punishing disciplinary infractions, and at the time Tannenbaum was writing, these included the dark cell, handcuffing, straitjackets, beatings, hanging from a door, or starvation for days at a time. Today, these include reclassification to higher security, disciplinary segregation, restrictions on visiting and programs, denial of parole or temporary absences, and the occasional diesel therapy.[2] What was particularly interesting is how the prison environment enabled cruelty on the part of guards by isolating them from convicts and emphasizing their authority to enforce all of the disciplinary rules of the institution.

Tannenbaum contrasted the "old system" of penitentiary management with reforms introduced by Thomas Mott Osborne, which emphasized prisoner welfare leagues and convict self-management. Relying upon interviews with convicts that Tannenbaum conducted both inside and outside Auburn and Sing Sing penitentiaries, Frank proceeded to describe the impact of the welfare league upon convicts. Most prisoners, even the professional gangsters, were positively affected by the experience of self-government.

In a precursor to his 1938 textbook, Tannenbaum (1922b) describes the development of the "professional criminal," one whom started as a juvenile delinquent often influenced by gang life and socially disorganized urban conditions. Failed by both home circumstances and the traditional schools, these boys spend a lot of unsupervised time on the streets with like-minded peers. Ultimately, he gets caught up in mischief or criminal activity, and gets apprehended by the authorities. After a few run-ins with the law, the youngster is sent to a juvenile institution. Here, Frank again relies upon his interviews with adult convicts. The average member of the public "would be startled at the tales of cruelty, barbarism, neglect, and mistreatment, which, if they were not so widely corroborated by practically all men who have been brought up in such institutions, would seem unbelievable" (Ibid.: p. 69). Frank quotes one professional criminal as saying:

I was sent to a juvenile institution at the age of eleven, and returned at about fifteen as a good pick-pocket. I went to a reformatory at seventeen as a pickpocket, and returned as a burglar, with all that implies in one's life and habits. As a burglar, I went to a state institution, where I acquired all the professional characteristics of the criminal and have since committed all the crimes, I suppose, which most criminals commit, and expect to end my life as a criminal.

(Ibid., p. 70–71)

Tannenbaum describes the psychology of prison inmate democracy as having a major influence on the prison population for two simple reasons: most of the convicts are in the same material position, and because they are incarcerated, they are more susceptible to peer influences, which they cannot easily escape. The prisoners' welfare league offered opportunity for programs, help with family problems, roles in self-government, and a means to lessen the pains of imprisonment

(Johnson & Toch, 1982). In Sing Sing, for example, Tannenbaum reported that on a prisoner's arrival, he was

> ... visited by a committee [of convicts] who interviewed him and found out what service they could render him. Was there anything he wanted to learn—was there any particular job that he could do best, or would like to do? Was there anything that the prison organization could do to help his family?
>
> (Ibid., pp. 81–82).

From the very outset in a maximum security prison, the existence of a prisoner's welfare league established a very different social atmosphere—one that had meaningful consequences for the inmate population. Frank recorded that the "boys in Sing Sing spoke of the prison as a college for the remaking of men. The boys in Portsmouth [Naval Prison] spoke of it as the University of Portsmouth" (Ibid., p. 87).

Nevertheless, Tannenbaum was a realist about the American prison system, based on his tour of 70 prisons during the summer of 1920. He wrote (Ibid., pp. 100–101):

> It is typical of the order and the discipline in prison—of the system, regularity, formalism, and, too frequently, of the silence. There is no spiritual life in the average American prison. There is no hope, no inspiration, no stimulus, no compulsion of the soul to better things.

The "old system" had no interest in the reforms put forward by Thomas Mott Osborne, and in fact, had deposed Osborne himself. Indeed, it was still characterized by outdated cell blocks, substandard health care, the absence of work, slavelike wages (where they even existed), and ineffectual educational programs. The casual observer might further remark that this continues to be a condition of prisons, especially in North America.

In the last chapter in *Wall Shadows*, Tannenbaum makes various suggestions for improving the American prison system. He begins with a recommendation that wardens be appointed, not for their politics, but for their training and education background and preferably those with college educations. Frank became more radical by arguing that the entire architecture of the prison system be scrapped in favor of prison farms, schools, factories, playgrounds—"almost anything different will be better" (Ibid., p. 141). In the South, Tannenbaum found hundreds of convicts working on prison farms, and thus questioned the utility of the old cellblock buildings.

> A large [tract] of land, a big farm, small barracks, plenty of sunshine and air, and the money for education and for health, for the building of character—these are substitutes for the raising of useless and perverting stone and iron cages, where men may confine their equals for deeds which they themselves might have committed if placed in their fellows' circumstances. Professionalization of prison administration and the destruction of the present prison buildings are essentials in any programme for prison reform. But they are only beginnings.
>
> (Ibid., p. 147)

Here, Frank believed, the existing penal departments should be abolished. Matters of punishment and incarceration should instead be administered by departments dedicated to education, health, and industry (p. 148). Convicts should be properly classified and designated to institutions best suited for their backgrounds. Hence, these new penal farms should be properly funded so that inmates have adequate health care, paid prison work, and suitable educational initiatives. Tannenbaum fully supported the notion of the indeterminate sentence and the granting of parole—then policies very much in vogue among penologists. In fact, he quotes wardens that he interviewed to the effect that "one half of the prison population could be released without proportionately endangering the safety of the community" (Ibid., p. 166). Finally, Frank strongly endorsed his mentor's program of prison democracy—even though he was well aware that Thomas Mott Osborn's reforms had been ignored or reversed across the country.

Shortly after publication of his *Wall Shadows*, Tannenbaum (1922c) wrote a nondescript article in an Anglican publication ostensibly about the obligation of the Church toward prisons and prisoners. This article was based on Frank's tour of Southern prisons where he came upon a cage of Black death-row inmates who were fervently singing "Nearer, My God to Thee." But the article was more than a call for religious action. It represented his initial thinking about the now-famous "dramatization of evil" thesis.

In this 1922 article, Tannenbaum (1922c: 13) described the prisoner as one

> . . . at the bottom of the social pyramid. He is the most helpless. There is no one below him. The tramp, the vagabond, the faker,

the beggar, the thief, the prostitute, the unskilled and verbatim . . . The man who has committed a crime becomes a criminal—not only the one thing he did but as a whole. We take the act of the man and plaster all of him with it. We say, *he* is a thief. That is not true. We ought to say that he committed a *theft*. . . We forget that he is a human being—a weak, an unfortunate, a misguided human being—but human still in spite . . . of the specific unsocial act he committed.

(Ibid.)

Citing Biblical terms, Tannenbaum argued that the criminal was formed and created in the community. "For if we do not provide the means of growth and development for socially desirable and useful men and women our neglect and indifference further the growth of graceless miscreants who practise the evil they have learned" (Ibid.). In a reverse of common logic, Frank wrote: "Every prison condemns the community that built it rather than the convicts it houses" (Ibid.). In a preview to what would later be known as labeling theory, Tannenbaum observed:

It is a startling fact that the mass of our law breakers are young men—mostly boys who are hardly out of their teens; that the mass of men who become professional criminals begin their careers as children in misfortune—children whose family is disrupted by death, disease, accident or sickness; that these children of six, seven, eight, and nine are sent to institutions where they get their drive, their mental attitude, their point of view, their perverted ideals, and their technique; that having once been committed to an institution, the community takes the form of an organized conspiracy to recommit them—to send them back.

(Ibid.)

Based on his own experiences in jail, Tannenbaum noted that prison administrations, with their host of rules, literally induce men to break the rules "if the men are to endure the existence the prison demands" (Ibid.). This necessarily creates a cycle of repression and revolt between the prison administration and the convicts.

Upon release, the ex-convict's isolation does not cease. His or her return is not welcomed. Respectable people "shun him. The police persecute him. The employers will not give him a job when they know him. The courts will not take his word in evidence. He is friendless, helpless, and bitter" (Ibid., p. 14). Finally, Tannenbaum indicts the Church as well.

> It claims him as its own special responsibility—to visit the imprisoned is its avowed obligation, but its visits are superficial and its work is of little significance in the lives of the half million souls that are confined in our penal institutions.
>
> (Ibid.)

Tannenbaum then undertook a tour of prison conditions in the American Deep South. In 1923, Tannenbaum published an article in *The Century Magazine*, which he included in his upcoming monograph, *Darker Phases of the South* (1924). He described the various forms of torture used on the chain gang, in prison farms, and by the convict-lease system (coal mining)—all parts of institutional policy and culture. Most of these penal facilities were disproportionately occupied by Southern Blacks, or "the color line" as Tannenbaum (1923a: 390) described it. Hunger and unsanitary conditions were structural components of the Southern prison system. Tuberculosis and syphilis were common medical conditions among the inmates. Tannenbaum had no real solution for reform except to reiterate the work of his mentor, Thomas Mott Osborne—who by then had been relieved of his prison reform work. He lamented the absence of a national program for prison reform, but did not indict the very nature of state's rights, which generated many of the dismal conditions he had seen in his visits. Nor did he locate institutional racism in an effort by white elites to maintain the "color line," cheap labor, and economic inequality. Later with the publication of *The Slave and Citizen* in 1947, Tannenbaum downplayed any economic analysis of slavery (Box 18, Slave & Citizen folder, letter to Emil Shuloff, dated March 21, 1946):

> Our race problem is not primarily economic, perhaps not even essentially economic . . . It is the fact that the tradition of the negro is a slave by nature that has hung over the American attitude which makes the problem.

Indeed, Frank was hostile not only to Eric Williams' neo-Marxist analysis in *Capitalism and Slavery* (1944), but also Gunnar Myrdal's *American Dilemma* (1944), arguing that comparisons about structural poverty should be made among Negroes themselves and not with white society (Tannenbaum, 1944).

Instead, Tannenbaum's thesis in *Slave and Citizen* was built around the notion of difference in the status and treatment of slaves in Central and South America, when contrasted to the history of slavery in the United States. Slaves in the United States were denied equality by law (the right to vote, marry, own property), but also a "moral status," which emphasized their subhuman status. By contrast, slavery was a prominent feature of the Iberian Peninsula, but their assimilation into society was not as hampered by legal or moral barriers. Slaves had the right to marry, purchase their freedom, and even complain of abusive treatment. These rights set the stage for the abolishment of slavery in Central and South America and the gradual elimination of the "color line" south of the American border.

In a response to Frank's *Century* article, then-governor of Arizona George W. Hunt wrote to the publisher of the magazine with these comments (Box 3, Folder H, Letter dated July 23, 1923):

> I think our prison system is probably our greatest crime against civilization, aside from war. Instead of curing morally and physically diseased persons and correcting weaknesses in human character, we take those who violate the law and put them through an intensive course in criminal education, and then turn them loose upon the world. Many of them are destined for an almost immediate return.

However, Hastings Hart, a consultant in penology for the Russell Sage Foundation in New York City, was more critical. In a March 20, 1923, letter to Frank, he argued that Tannenbaum's article had painted a biased picture of both prison wardens and prison conditions in the South. He then proceeded to outline modest improvements in various prison systems—illustrating the difference in opinion between a convict perspective and that of a professional consultant to those very correctional agencies (Box 3, Folder H).

Even the executive director of the National Committee on Prisons and Labor criticized Frank for this overly negative portrayal of Southern prisons (Box 5, Folder W, letter of April 24, 1923).

Notes

1 Indeed, Max Horkheimer and other members of the Frankfurt School of critical theory had immigrated to the United States around 1934, eventually settling at Columbia University as the International Institute of Social Research (McCole, Benhabib, & BonB, 1993: 7). Columbia University Press published Rusche and Kirchheimer's

Punishment and Social Structure in 1939, and yet there is no evidence of any contact between Tannenbaum and Kirchheimer. In 1964, there was some limited contact between Tannenbaum and Max Horkheimer over the translation of *Crime and the Community* into German (Box 31, Crime & Folder, Letter to Mr. Bruegelmann dated July 22, 1964).

2   This refers to spending time in transit on buses or airplanes, shackled from head to toe, and sometimes confined to small cages.

7

BECOMING A PUBLIC
INTELLECTUAL

In response to a question about how he felt about the problems of the
unemployed in 1925, Frank had this to say (Robinson, 1925):

> I have broadened considerably since then. I have added many
> things to my intellectual make-up. In 1914, I was convinced I
> had the key to heaven and that no one else's key would fit the
> lock. Now I know that others will.
>
> I am still a Socialist. The social problem is not a Gordian
> knot that can be cut by one sweep of the sword. In 1914 we had
> great unemployment. So far as unemployment is concerned, to
> permit starvation is a greater crime than is the property crime
> of stealing. It's not only criminal but preposterously stupid. I
> believe that society ought to provide the unemployed man with
> an opportunity to make his own bread with the sweat of his brow.
> However, I think it is pretty definite that we are progressing.

Frank Tannenbaum would later obtain his doctorate from the Brookings Institution in 1927 under the general rubric of "The Mexican
Agricultural System." Of interest, initially he had proposed to write
his dissertation on the professional criminal. By 1922, Tannenbaum
had already made one trip to Mexico to study labor organizations and
what he deemed a "miracle school" located in a Mexico City slum on
behalf of *Century Magazine* (Tannenbaum, 1923b). By 1925, he had
decided to pursue the subject of Mexican land reform, and had begun
graduate studies at the Robert Brookings Graduate School of Economics and Government in Washington, D.C. The school awarded
him a fellowship of $1,000 to begin his studies (Box 3, Folder H, Letter
of March 5, 1926). Since 1910, Mexico had held a special place of
interest among American radicals, who followed the revolution

intently. His dissertation was later published as *The Mexican Agrarian Revolution* in 1929. For his research, Tannenbaum had spent over a year in Mexico, collecting data and interviewing prominent authorities—much to the consternation of U.S. authorities who considered him a radical and anti-American. By this time, July 1928, Tannenbaum had accepted a part-time staff position with the Brookings Institution (Box 3, folder M(2), appointment letter of July 16, 1928).

Even during this period, Tannenbaum continued speaking to various groups on the subject of prison reform. One speech before Syracuse University faculty and the League of Women Voters was recorded by the Syracuse *Post-Standard*, November 22, 1926. The paper noted:

> American prisons, instead of reforming convicts, turn out men, the majority of whom return as "repeaters" at some time in their later lives, according to Frank Tannenbaum, student of crime and labor conditions.
>
> Tannenbaum declared statistics show 70 percent of those released convicts return to prisons on new charges later. The treatment a man receives from police, courts, and prison attendants makes him more rather than less likely to commit further offenses, he said.
>
> Thomas Mott Osborne of Auburn who died recently, Mr. Tannenbaum praised as a rare example of a man who was able to treat criminals as men fundamentally and not to look down upon them.
>
> The speaker made the point that the difference between a criminal and a respected citizen is often slight and declared that "if everybody who had ever committed a deed for which someone, sometime, has been sent to prison, most every person would have served behind bars at some time or another."

It is worth noting that Tannenbaum even had a publicity agent, Louis Alber, who helped him orchestrate paid speaking engagements (Box 2, Letter from L. Alber, November 14, 1923, Folder A). He was also on tour with the Swarthmore Chautauqua Association of Pennsylvania as a paid speaker (Box 4, Folder P&Q). Later, in 1928, Tannenbaum was promoted as a lecturer by the Sterling Artists Bureau of Los Angeles, California (Box 4, Folder S(2), Letter of July 30, 1928).

On the subject of prison riots, Tannenbaum concluded that they "did not materialize from temporary circumstances . . . but resulted from the effects of a system termed archaic and incompetent as to its moral, social, and administrative aspects" (*North Adams Evening Transcript,* Williamstown, Massachusetts, August 10, 1929, p. 2).

> The whole penological system should concern itself basically and continuously with the task of reconstructing the criminal . . . and to date, this aspect of our prisons, far from being a dominant interest, has been a complete and total failure. The principle responsibility of our prison system should not be revenge. It should be to develop and change the life interests of the so-called criminal.
>
> At present, he said, prisoners of all sorts of mental and moral standards are herded in crowded and unsanitary cells and their principle occupation is to feed on their past experiences or to construct a new life built on that past experience. Under these conditions, the prison becomes an instrument for perpetuating the prisoners' past and even giving it greater emotional intensity.

The stress of Tannenbaum's numerous book projects and his studies and travel for the Brookings Institution caused his marriage to Esther Tannenbaum to crumble. Frank would file for and be granted a divorce in Sonora, Mexico, on June 27, 1929 (Box 5, Folder T(2), original divorce decree in Spanish). She would remarry Mr. Elaihu Hurwitz on July 18, 1929, and both children were later adopted in Bronx County Surrogate's Court circa June 9, 1931.[1] Born in Russia and having immigrated to the United States circa 1911, Mr. Hurwitz was actually trained as a pharmacist but spent most of his career as an insurance salesman. For her part, Esther remained a housewife following her second marriage. Zalkind "Ziggy" Hurwitz would become a well-respected musician and arranger during his career, who operated a piano studio in Charlotte, North Carolina. He passed away in 1994. Nessa took care of her mother, who suffered a stroke in 1947 that paralyzed her right side. Following her mother's death in 1957, Nessa would marry a Mr. Julius Sternfeld and occupy herself as a public relations and publication executive until her recent death in 2011. Eli Hurwitz passed away in 1968 at the age of 76.

As early as 1928, Tannenbaum signed a contract with a publisher from New York City, Thomas Crowell Company, to write a book on penal administration. That book was never delivered, but subsequently became *Crime and the Community* (1938) a decade later (Tannenbaum Collection, Box 2, Folder E. Butler Library, Columbia U). By 1933,

Tannenbaum had written a chapter for the book, in which he criticized the prevailing individual pathology model in criminology (Box 2, Folder E, correspondence dated August 3, 1933 to Seba Eldridge of the University of Kansas).

Nevertheless, Tannenbaum continued to agitate for prison reform. In August 1929, he was invited to address the Virginia Institute of Public Affairs, then holding a conference in Charlottesville. "Our whole present penal system is repressive," he declared. "It leads to distortion and perversion of human character. It will never be successful until it constructs a new basis for individuals' future happiness in society" (Dunlap, 1929). Here, he suggested than once the convict is sentenced, he or she should be properly classified and then dealt with "by other administrative departments, such as those of health , educational, and labor." In blunt terms, departments of corrections were unredeemable failures and their jurisdiction should cease.

But starting in 1929, Tannenbaum was looking for another project and asked his friend, Felix Frankfurter, then at the Harvard University Law School, to make introductions on his behalf to the secretary of the Wickersham Commission, Mr. Max Lowenthal. This resulted in Tannenbaum becoming the reporter in March 1931 of Volume 9 of the Wickersham Commission reports, titled *Report on Penal Institutions, Probation and Parole* (Box 1, Correspondence of Felix Frankfurter, June 3, 1929). As noted by historian David Rothman (1980), Tannenbaum had become a well-known expert on American prisons, not only due to his early survey of prisons in 1920, but also as a result of his book *Wall Shadows* in 1922. His confinement as a convict in 1914 to 1915 clearly shaped Tannenbaum's perspective on prisons, and were known to the members of the commission themselves.

The result of this volume of the Wickersham Commission became front-page news across America (*New York Times,* July 27, 1931). The report attacked the construction and maintenance of fortresslike penitentiaries, such as Auburn, New York, and ended:

> We conclude that the present prison system is antiquated and inefficient. It does not reform the criminal. It fails to protect society. There is reason to believe that it contributes to the increase of crime by hardening the prisoner.

As a drafter, Tannenbaum documented various disciplinary punishments at the time, some of which included shackling men to doors, whipping them, water torture techniques, confinement to small cages, and long periods in dark cells with only bread and water. As a result, the report documented numerous riots, fires, murders, the presence of drugs in prisons, and "the frequent atmosphere of hate and bitterness" (Ibid.).

In calling for numerous reforms, commission members were undoubtedly more conservative than Tannenbaum. They recommended better classification of prisoners, actual wages to be paid to convicts, the abolition of torture, educational programs, expansion of parole, the use of suspended sentences (probation) in lieu of prison, and the elimination of the exploitive contract system of prison labor.

Of great relevance, upon the release of this report, Tannenbaum created a furor at the annual congress of the American Prison Association, then meeting in Baltimore, Maryland, on October 23, 1931 (Associated Press, 1931). At that meeting, Tannenbaum characterized the report as "a mild, friendly document when it ought to be a severe and unrelenting indictment of the present penal system and all its doings." To quote a copy of Tannenbaum's speech to the congress (Box 31, Criminology Folder No. 2):

> I am saying nothing new, but merely repeating what has been said a thousand times before by people of all degrees and in a thousand places, that imprisonment makes people worse rather than better. Not only should no man be sent to prison except as a last resort, but no man ought to be kept in prison a day longer than is absolutely essential for the safety of society. And the prison which stands between the convicted man and his ultimate return to society ought to be an institution that is dedicated to the reconstruction of individual character.
>
> I agree with Dr. George W. Kirchway in his statement that the report of the Wickersham Commission on Penal Institutions suffers by being too conservative, too generous, in its estimate of the present penal institution. I agree with him that the report is a mild, friendly document when it ought to be a severe and unrelenting indictment of the present penal system and all of its doings. I am therefore going to amend the report. I am going to add some of the elements which he finds lacking in it.

He mentioned the 1930 fire at an Ohio prison that killed 317 convicts, describing the situation as political jockeying, indifference, and incompetence. When it was suggested that the warden resign, this individual replied that his critics were only trying to encourage "the Bolshevist element." It was vintage Tannenbaum, the Tannenbaum of his youth when he was a member of the Industrial Workers of the World (IWW). He described various means of torture inflicted on some 200 prisoners in segregation at the prison in Clinton, New York, circa 1929, after a riot. He described the aftermath of a riot at the state prison in Missouri in March 1930, in which beatings were administered by guards to about 75 convicts. In conclusion, Tannenbaum stated:

> We behave as though we believed that cruelty and fear and physical pain would lead to kindness, gentleness, co-operation and good citizenship on the part of the released prisoners. That's not true. Cruelty begets cruelty, hardness begets hardness, and lack of kindness is paid in the same token . . . The penal institution must be considered as providing a great educational opportunity for the community, to redeem and reconstruct, the unsocial elements that have been segregated there.

As a result, the American Prison Association ended up approving a resolution endorsing the Wickersham report, when originally there had been rumblings by various "progressive" wardens to protest the findings (*New York Times*, October, 23, 1931; *Washington Post,* 1931). During the early 1930s, Tannenbaum continued to agitate for prison reform and wrote complaints to various prison agencies.

Later, circa November 1934, Tannenbaum wrote a report for the President's Commission on Prison Industries (known as the Ulman Commission, for the chairman, Joseph Ulman, who was a judge in Baltimore). The impetus for this study group was a dispute between the Southern cotton garment industry and the Prison Labor Authority of President Roosevelt's National Recovery Administration, circa late 1933.[2] In April 1935, President Roosevelt signed an executive order announcing a "Fair Competition" pact between various state prison industries and the private sector. This agreement, made during the Depression and at a time when prison populations were bulging (Bennett, 1935), allowed state correctional facilities to sell convict goods on the open market in clear competition with the private sector. Tannenbaum, of course, had come to the attention of the White House due to the publication of *Osborne of Sing Sing*, in which Roosevelt had written the introduction.

Tannenbaum and members of the committee concluded that prison idleness was a major security problem that not only made prisons dangerous and prone to riots, but undermined efforts at rehabilitation for the 94 percent of inmates who would eventually be released. But because major industries were opposed to the pact, the committee compromised and opted to support a state-use system for prison products (National Recovery Administration, 1934). The Ulman Commission then recommended that the federal government appropriate at least $50 million dollars to encourage state prison systems to end chain gangs and facilitate state prison industries that would address rehabilitation and idleness. Part of this idea was to encourage the manufacture of prison-made items that could be sold to government agencies and would give convicts training, labor, and a wage while confined. Hence, states would need to pass "state-use" laws to protect markets for prison products. Indeed, this committee suggested that prisoners could be used in road building, school furniture, and printing—labor that previously had been barred to convicts. Under this plan, various state prison systems could buy in to federal funding with a matching grant. This report became the basis for an executive order (No. 7194) and subsequent legislation creating the Prison Industries Reorganization Administration during 1935. A key plank of this legislation prohibited interstate transportation of prison-made goods to those states that had outlawed prison products. In fact, Frank was appointed a consultant of the new agency (Box 42, Prison Industries Committee Folder, Appointment of April 8, 1936). Despite this effort and Tannenbaum's long-time interest in improving prison labor for convicts, the fledgling agency was not popular with members of Congress and their business constituents, and was closed for lack of appropriations in 1938 (Flynn, 1950). During its existence, the agency had evaluated and made recommendations in 25 states and operated on a paltry budget of $50,000.

By the onset of the 1930s, Tannenbaum no longer associated with his comrades from the IWW. He seemed more content to pursue the life of an academic, speaker, and contract researcher, particularly on issues affecting Mexico and land reform. As we will see later, this quite naturally created a theoretical void in his work on criminology. By early 1933, he even complained to friends that he was in financial straits, and was soliciting paid speaking engagements. By the 1940s, his radical views had changed dramatically. In the 1946 issue of the *Political Science Quarterly*, Tannenbaum would be highly critical of communist societies, class struggle, and Marxism in general. Instead, he endorsed market democracy in which there is a "balance of the social institutions," specifically the family, the church, and the state (Tannenbaum, 1946: 501). "Conflict, strife, divergence, difference of interest and opinion over many things for many reasons, and in varying degrees of intensity, are the conditions of social peace. The conflicting processes of democracy are consistent with and essentially a part of the stresses and strains of life itself" (p. 504)

> But as soon as one of the institutions, be it the state, the church, the family or the economy, becomes so strong as seemingly to threaten the very survival of the others, then the issue cease to be petty, capable of compromise, and the arguments become preludes to civil wars and revolutions.
>
> (p. 500)

Hence, for Tannenbaum, the solution was to preserve a market society based on private capital and strengthen "those institutions that seemed to be losing ground" (p. 501).

In private correspondence, Tannenbaum was critical of a centralized state ("what we call socialism") and opted instead to strengthen local institutions, such as the "shop, the union, and the local parish" (Box 7, Folder D, Letter to Russell Davenport dated October 4, 1951). In an interview that appeared in the *New York Times* (Breit, 1951), Tannenbaum had this to say:

> I believe in a world where there is a great deal of power at the local level, at the bottom, at the community, like a pyramid. What we've done is reverse it: the power is on top, the weakness at the bottom. Russia is the best example of that. We must go back to communities.

In July 1935, Frank secured a lecturer position at Columbia, and from the very beginning, opted to specialize in Latin American history (*Bayonne Times,* 1935).[3] Previously, he had taught at Cornell University in the summer of 1932, where he gave courses on criminology, as well as at Yale University in the summer of 1934. Only two years later in April 1937, he was promoted to tenured faculty (associate professor) in the Department of Political Science, still specializing in Latin American history. In April 1945, he was made full professor of Latin American history, and by this time, had formally moved to the History Department. He remained at Columbia until retiring in 1961 as professor emeritus of

Latin American history, and continued as director of the university seminars, which he originated in 1944.[4] Frank would host a weekly Latin American seminar in Spanish attended by many intellectuals, writers, ambassadors, and journalists until his death in 1969. Indeed, at Columbia University, there is a seminar room named after him called the Frank Tannenbaum room.

Figure 7.1 Frank's official 1940s university photo at Columbia

Figure 7.2 Frank's official 1938 photo as a new professor at Columbia University

Notes

1 Surrogate's Court for Bronx County, State of New York, File Nos. 77X-1931 & 78X-1931. Order of Judge A. Henderson.
2 Correspondence from R. W. Lea, Administrator, National Recovery Administration to Marvin McIntyre (White House), dated November 8, 1933. Official file 459 "Prisons," Franklin D. Roosevelt Presidential Library, Hyde Park, New York.

3 Appointment Records, 1890s–1990, Box UA#134, Columbia University Archives, Butler Library, Rare Book and Manuscript Library.
4 The Columbia University seminars were founded by Professor Tannenbaum (1953, 1965) in 1944 as a means to facilitate dialogue on special topics by bringing together a host of individuals, academics, diplomats, politicians, and students to keep abreast of special topics (Jaquith, 1973).

8

CRIME AND THE COMMUNITY

As noted previously, Tannenbaum had signed a book contract to write on the subject of crime and the professional criminal. This project actually started with a small article in the publication *The Standard*, published by the American Ethical Union of New York City under the tutelage of Felix Adler. In an early sample of his thinking, Tannenbaum (1924b: 87) argued that criminals, and especially the professional, were made—much like "lawyers, doctors and professors are made." By the term "professional," Tannenbaum was really referring to recidivists. He rejected the then-prevalent notion of biological or genetic deformity that dominated mainstream criminology. Instead, he preferred to concentrate on peer contacts and habit-forming patterns—obviously based on his own incarceration and conversations with numerous convicts in prison.

As a rule, the recidivist or professional criminal came from a broken, inadequate home. "This leads, in early childhood, to an overemphasis on the importance of street life and gang associations" (Tannenbaum, 1924b: 88).

> The ideals of the gang become a central and dominating influence in the development of his habits of life. These ideals and attitudes are nurtured by contacts with other boys and young men who have had similar experiences and deprivations in early life.

Often, group delinquency results in arrest and processing by law enforcement and subsequent commitment to a foster or group home. This institutionalization contributes to the maintenance of a counterculture where the boy demonstrates a "natural suspicion of all the older and authoritative persons in the institution" (Ibid.). Upon his release, he is isolated and, in fact, ostracized by his peers. He thereupon finds companionship with other peers, many of whom have similar class and criminal justice trajectories. Upon the commission of further delinquencies, the teenager is committed to a reformatory. "He develops a philosophy of life that centers about the assumption that all people are bad and that he is only different because he has been caught" (Ibid., p. 89). Upon release, his attitudes have hardened. Frank quotes one of the convicts he met in prison: "After you have been in prison as long as I have you don't care what you do to other people."

But Tannenbaum was interested in the impact of the prison upon the delinquent or adult criminal. It results in an overemphasis on some emotional experiences that results in a "remembered hate," a desire for revenge for some injury or betrayal.

> The prison thus makes the criminal's career almost inevitable by giving the prisoner nothing of interest in current experience, and in this way compels him to over-emphasize the vivid emotional interests of his past life, thereby making a return to them almost a foregone conclusion.

In a follow-up to this short article on the professional criminal, Tannenbaum (1924c) reviewed five books for the December 1924 issue of *The Standard*. One of the books he reviewed was a monograph by an American female convict, Kate Richard O'Hare (1923), which provided personal testimony to the cruel treatment of women prisoners. O'Hare was a prominent socialist who was convicted of allegedly inciting citizens to oppose enlistment for World War I. Another book was authored by a British prison inspector of women's prisons named Mary Gordon (1922). Tannenbaum was so impressed with her findings that he quoted her text:

> During my service I found nothing in the prison system to interest me, except as a gigantic irrelevance—a social curiosity. If the system had a good effect on any prisoner, I failed to mark it. I have no doubt of its power to demoralize, or of its cruelty. It appears to me not to belong to this time or civilization at all.
>
> My main argument here is that we not only do not deter, but that we do actually make over our criminal to crime. The fallacy of applying force to a being who is inherently insusceptible to being managed by force, lies in the fact that the proceeding ends, not in the alteration of the prisoner's point of view, but in his spiritually triumphing over us, and the bringing of the strong

CRIME AND THE COMMUNITY

arm of the law to naught. We merely ill-treat a man or woman who still ignores and escapes us.

(Tannenbaum, 1924c: 124–125)

Of course, Tannenbaum would expand upon the theme of the professional criminal with an article in *Century Magazine*. This article would later be incorporated into his 1938 monograph; but in 1925, Tannenbaum was interested explaining the development of professional criminality. Here he argued that "[t]he community gives the criminal his materials and habits, just as it gives the doctor, the lawyer, the teacher, and the candlestick-maker theirs" (Tannenbaum, 1925: 577). In an early precursor to Sutherland's theory of differential association, Tannenbaum expounded on the nature of habit formation.

It is significant that the professional criminal comes from an insufficient home. It is frequently a broken home. Frequently, there is a dead father, a dead mother, sickness, disease, drunkenness, poor moral standards, internal conflict, lack of family discipline, lack of family interest. Where the home is insufficient, the child takes the street as a substitute for the home. The street gang [becomes] the place for more than adventure; it becomes the place of escape from the home.

(Tannenbaum, 1925: 580–581)

Tannenbaum further observed that the two distinguishing features of the early career of professional criminals were (1) a breakdown in their family circumstances, and (2) early imprisonment in a reformatory. Here, Tannenbaum laments that the real story of what happens in juvenile institutions "is yet to be told." Burdened by large populations and few resources, the common denominator for institutional discipline becomes the infliction of corporal punishment. Upon his return to his nuclear family, nothing has changed. Except now, the young lad has picked up a neighborhood label to the effect: "Don't play with Billy. Billy is a bad boy. He has been up at the juvenile" (Tannenbaum, 1925: 583). This entire process results in the formation of subculture networks, often around gangs. The police, the courts, and the prisons become not only a regulatory system, but one that keeps "the man bound to his world of crime" (Tannenbaum, 1925: 586).

It is perhaps not too much to say that the prison is the chief reason for the continuance of the criminal career, for the return of

85

CRIME AND THE COMMUNITY

the criminal to his previous haunt. The fact that approximately seventy-five percent of the professional criminals are known to be recidivists . . . is sufficient proof that confinement does not keep them from returning.

(Tannenbaum, 1925: 586)

Indeed, Frank proposed a book on penal administration as early as October 1928, just after finishing his dissertation at the Brookings Institution in Washington, D.C., in correspondence to Professor Seba Eldridge of the University of Kansas, who represented a publishing company. Originally, Frank did not like the titles of "Penology" or "Criminology," because he was " not at all certain that I know what they mean when examined in the light of the practices and procedure that are covered by those names" (Box 2, Folder E, Letter to Prof. Eldridge, November 13, 1928). Tannenbaum also lobbied Eldridge to obtain additional funds from the publisher so that he could tour American penitentiaries, like he did during the summer of 1920. The book contract with Thomas Y. Crowell Company of New York City was signed in November 1928, but did not include the sought-after travel funds (Box 2, Folder E).

This book project percolated for several years, until 1933–1935, while Tannenbaum was still a staff member of the Brookings Institution under the general title, *Reconstructing Criminal Behavior*. Tannenbaum now devoted himself to this project, incorporating portions of his previous work for the Wickersham Commission, his just-published book on Thomas Mott Osborne, and his analysis of the professional criminal. We know that Edwin Sutherland was extremely critical of the proposed book and wrote a five-page diatribe to Professor Seba Eldridge of the University of Kansas on August 4, 1935 (Tannenbaum collection, Box 31, Criminology Folder—II). This was interesting because Sutherland quoted extensively from Tannenbaum's *Wall Shadows* in his own 1924 textbook, called simply, *Criminology*.

In that letter, Sutherland stated that the most serious objection was a lack of balance on the part of Tannenbaum. "[T]he student will get no appreciation of many of the approaches to the causation of delinquency and crime; he will get an appreciation only of the particular approach which Tannenbaum favors." Sutherland observed that Tannenbaum places almost exclusive emphasis on the "developed gang boy," and then suggests that—a clear precursor to his famous work on white-collar crime—"the most dangerous 'criminals' in America are of the Insull-Mitchell-Wiggins-Van Sweringen type, who were characteristically

86

CRIME AND THE COMMUNITY

well behaved as boys, but developed their fraudulent methods in the culture of the business world" (p. 1). Sutherland further complained that the proposed manuscript was too wordy, badly written, and not up-to-date with respect to certain facts about the U.S. prison system. Whereas Tannenbaum critiqued the contemporary assumptions about qualitative differences between criminals and noncriminals, Sutherland noted some backsliding in his treatment of truants, since Tannenbaum noted several psychological characteristics as important.

Sutherland further questioned Tannenbaum's notion of the professional criminal by first arguing that "a professional criminal is much less likely to be followed by imprisonment than the crime of an occasional offender, and that the big-shot professional criminals spend very little time in prisons." After providing detailed notes about various manuscript corrections, Sutherland abruptly changed his tone in the same letter:

> I wish to say in general that this manuscript contains the best statement I have seen of the social psychology of crime; this appears especially on page 18 where it is subordinated to the analysis of the gang. The same statements would apply in much more general sense to any kind of delinquency.
>
> I wish to state, also, that Tannenbaum is always a very stimulating and suggestive writer. Some parts of this book remind me more of a book of essays than of a text book. I doubt whether it will appeal to many teachers and especially whether it will hold the interest of teachers for very long. But it will certainly, if published somewhat as present, be read with much interest and parts of it will be regarded as extraordinarily good.

Crime and the Community would not be published until 1938 when Frank was well ensconced as an associate professor in history at Columbia. Published by Ginn and Company, the book was quite different from the typical criminology textbook of the day.

Frank spent the first chapter arguing that the "criminal" was often a scapegoat for causes embedded in the community. As we will see later, those causes were often structural to the extent that they were part of the political economy of urban America.

Like his mentor, Thomas Mott Osborne, Tannenbaum criticized the prevailing positivist approach to criminality, suggesting that the theories of Cesare Lombroso (1911) and Havelock Ellis (1910) were

Figure 8.1 Frank Tannenbaum in his Columbia University office, circa 1950

fundamentally wrong. He even observed that the shift away from criminological anthropology (particularly its emphasis on physiology) to internal psychological notions of "possession" or "evil" were equally deficient. Influenced by the Chicago School of sociology, Tannenbaum instead argued that crime "is a maladjustment that arises out of the conflict between a group and the community at large" (1938: 8). He would further contend that the derivation of these group conflicts has its origins in the very social structure, history, and political economy of urban society.

CRIME AND THE COMMUNITY

In the meantime, urban delinquency was heavily associated with play groups, often called gangs, that formed in downtown neighborhoods characterized by high mobility, poverty, unemployment, failed schools, crowding, immigrant housing, street crime, and even professional syndicate crime (Thrasher, 1927). The response of official institutions, like the beat policeman and the truant officer, was to "criminalize" behaviors that previously were ignored or considered nuisances, not crimes. This naturally led to Tannenbaum's now-famous "Dramatization of Evil" thesis (1938: 19–20):

> The process of making the criminal, therefore, is a process of tagging, defining, identifying, segregating, describing, emphasizing, making conscious and self-conscious; it becomes a way of stimulating, suggesting, emphasizing, and evoking the very traits that are complained of.
>
> The child's isolation forces him into companionship with other children similarly defined, and the gang becomes his means of escape, his security.

This commentary in Tannenbaum's book has since become historically important among labeling theorists, and it is Tannenbaum's best-known contribution to criminological theory (Cullen & Wilcox, 2010; Jacoby, Severance, & Bruce, 2012). The late Donald Cressey (1965) pointed out that Tannenbaum was likely the first American criminologist to address the labeling effect, and that his 1938 text had a major impact on American criminology in the work of Howard Becker (1963), David Matza (1969), William Chambliss (1973), Edwin Lemert (1951), and Edwin Schur (1973), among others.

Nevertheless, Tannenbaum insisted on contextualizing his group conflict thesis in urban political economy. In the several chapters that followed, he wrote (1938: 25) that "criminals are themselves part of the community in its deeper sense, and are as much its products as are its philosophers, poets, inventors, business men and scientists, reformers, and saints." Tannenbaum went on to document the history of the United States as one grounded in conflicts over land, immigration, class, labor, race, tribal rights, and development—all of which generated a pervasive "striving for success." He attributed much crime simply to the growth of the criminal law, largely as a result of industrialization and new conflicts over labor, health, and working standards. In major urban populations, this in turn was influenced by machine politics, the immigrant vote, and municipal corruption. To quote Frank

(1938: 35): "Therefore a partial answer to the question why we have had so much crime in the United States is to be found in the peculiar character of our urban politics."

To help explain chronic delinquency and professional crime, Tannenbaum alluded to the environment in urban America characterized by the fence, members of organized crime, older criminals, and the failures of legitimate institutions—like the schools, the church, and the factory. Here, Tannenbaum quoted not only his own interviews with delinquents (based on the Osborne correspondence), but the work of Chicagoans Clifford Shaw and Henry McKay (1931), to which he was exposed during his work for the Wickersham Commission. Part of the "hardening" process in a criminal career was the institutional experience a youngster had with imprisonment and reformatories. "The institutional experience is thus a concentration of stimuli adapted to develop delinquent interests" (1938: 71). Methodologically, Tannenbaum relied heavily upon his own experience at Blackwell's Island Penitentiary and the observations of other convicts. He was, indeed, utilizing a convict standpoint in not only debunking what he considered myths in criminology, but explaining the common delinquent's "education for crime."

The book's chapters on organized crime, politics, politics and the police, and finally the professional criminal serve to highlight the long-standing relationships between certain delinquent gangs, organized crime, and urban political machines. Here, a coterie of bail bondsmen, attorneys, fixers, and ward heelers exist to help sustain the underworld culture of the professional or career offender.

Tannenbaum was especially critical of two assumptions made by contemporary criminology during this era. The first was the notion that there exists a unitary cause of crime; and the second was the assumption that the individual is inherently criminal. Whether the explanation was based on Lombroso's criminal anthropology, or intelligence tests, or some innate psychological pathology, Tannenbaum found these theories wanting. "The idea of type, of normal, however, is a statistical construct. It has no existence in nature. To compare the prison population in terms of any set of personal traits with some imaginary norm which does not exist is to indulge in idle intellectual play that may not be entirely harmless" (1938: 212). To Tannenbaum and Thomas Mott Osborne, the so-called assumption of difference was largely a myth, conditioned by institutional demands to justify the processing of malefactors.

Tannenbaum's chapters on the penal system would reproduce much of his own early work and experience, particularly the influence of

CRIME AND THE COMMUNITY

Thomas Mott Osborne. He described the penal system up to the early 1930s as one based predominantly on the "old cell block" system. These institutions were often quite old, unsanitary, and overcrowded, and prisoners had few educational or labor options. Wardens tended to be political appointees, and guards were underpaid and poorly trained for their positions. To Frank, the entire penal system was a historic failure, and reforms such as Osborne's Mutual Welfare League had "been destroyed completely" (p. 433).

> It would be difficult to invent a more effective method for conditioning the criminal in his career than imprisoning him with some hundreds of other prisoners, each of whom has a tale of adventure, of pride, of success and of failure, of ends and plans, all in terms of the past career as a criminal and in terms of a future career in the same field.
>
> (p. 476)

Unfortunately, Tannenbaum had few suggestions for the future in the final chapter of *Crime and the Community*. He blithely argued that if the causes of crime are to be found in the nature and structure of "the community," then those factors must be addressed. This was essentially an argument in favor of political economy and the very structure of capital markets and urban politics. Unfortunately, by 1938, Frank Tannenbaum was reluctant to apply any set of theories, let alone those of his anarchist past, to explain the multiple causes of delinquency.

The reaction to *Crime and the Community* was quite favorable among the criminological community (Bain, 1938; Schulman, 1938; Vold, 1938; Meyer, 1939). Even Frankfurt School theorist Otto Kirchheimer (1938) gave the book a favorable nod without criticizing the book from the perspective of neo-Marxist theory (Rusche & Kirchheimer, 1939). Joseph Lohman (1939), then at the University of Chicago, wrote to request permission to use an excerpt from the book, and there was favorable reaction from Hans W. Mattick, then director of the Chicago Youth Development Project. To quote Mattick's commentary on the 1938 edition, reprinted in 1951 and 1961 without change (Tannenbaum Collection, Box 31, Memorandum dated February 15, 1963):

> The book *Crime and the Community* is, in my opinion, the best single text in criminology available today, and it is one of the best preparatory texts for those who would understand the social forces that shape the lives of youth in the inner-city.

So do not be put off by sources and quotations that are dated in the 1920's. Many of the same points made by Cloward and Ohlin, Edwin Sutherland, Al Cohen and Walter Miller were already present in this early text, and some of them have never been stated better than they were by Tannenbaum.

In 1940, Tannenbaum returned to a favorite theme in an address before the National Committee on Prisons and Prison Labor, with which he had been affiliated since the 1920s. Here, Frank argued for a differentiation between the "professional" criminal and the accidental offender, and that "the problem of crime is a problem that is confined to the professional criminal, that is, to the man who makes his living by committing crime" (Tannenbaum, 1940: 4).

He argued that the penitentiary was an inappropriate institution for the so-called nonprofessional. As a point of fact, Tannenbaum suggested that the juvenile reformatory and the adult penitentiary were formative institutions for the professional or career criminal.

> I am convinced that your juvenile institutions, reformatories and prisons tend to create . . . your major contributions to the creation of the attitude of mind, the philosophy of life of the professional criminal.
>
> (Tannenbaum, 1940: 5)

He further suggested that a focus on the individual convict historically has failed, and would continue to fail because such interventions did not address the street criminal's group allegiances. Tannenbaum felt that much juvenile delinquency should be ignored, or at least the minor infractions. Instead, he favored peer group interventions, and even suggested that reformers use labor unions, churches, and cellar clubs as a means of offering youth alternatives to delinquent behavior. He mentioned the work of Thomas Mott Osborne, who used the Mutual Welfare League as a means of changing institutional behavior among convicts. Of course, Frank never addressed where the funds to provide these other alternatives might originate and whether elite interests actually favored low tax rates and interstitial areas in urban centers that housed concentrations of immigrants, the poor, people of color, and underfunded social agencies.

In 1944, Tannenbaum was invited to write the foreword to Barnes and Tetters' *New Horizons in Criminology*. Tannenbaum had been in touch with Harry Elmer Barnes since early 1919 when Professor Barnes was on faculty at the New School for Social Research. Here, Tannenbaum (1944: v–viii) repeated his previous position dating back at least 25 years:

> Under these circumstances our problem becomes not the search for the impossible—the abolition of crime—but the quest for some possible means for its diminution and for the reshaping of the habit-patterns of individuals who become criminals. We have failed in both of these. Our methods of punishment ... do not reduce the number of crimes committed nor improve the way of life of the imprisoned. Recidivism is conspicuous, especially in those who were the first to be "reformed" by an initial incarceration. The prison is not a reformatory, and the reformatory is essentially a prison in spite of its name.
>
> The repudiation of imprisonment as the chief and almost the only method of dealing with the criminal is the only logical position to take. The prison does not solve the problem of crime—it only aggravates it and increases the number of practitioners addicted to illegal behavior as a way of life.

Although *Crime and the Community* was republished in 1951, and again in 1963 by Columbia University Press, the book had not been updated, and what could have been a major contribution to the field faded away as well (Vold, 1952). The highly regarded criminologist George B. Vold criticized the new reprint because many of the illustrations were pre–World War II and had not been properly updated. The U.S. federal prison system had expanded as well as numerous state reformatories and prison systems. In private correspondence, Vold also argued that the analogy of prison inmates as "hospital patients" was unsound. In Vold's view, inmates were more similar to "prisoners of war" (Box 28, Columbia University Press Folder, Letter of Vold to Tannenbaum, dated December 29, 1952).

> In the case of real prisoners of war, we do not expect the standard of living of the particular concentration camp to which such prisoners are sent to have much to do with whether they will remain loyal to their own national political ideology or whether they will change over to that of their captors.

Nevertheless, Vold felt that the book could be salvaged with a major effort made to updating its sources and observations. Tannenbaum

CRIME AND THE COMMUNITY

actually agreed with these observations and even asked Vold whether he would "interested in undertaking the revision." Unfortunately for the history of criminological thought, that revision never materialized.

Finally, it is part of our cultural history that in the TV show *Ironside*, actor Raymond Burr tells one of his helpers, "Go to the library and get Frank Tannenbaum's *Crime and the Community*" (Tannenbaum Papers, Box 28, Columbia University Press Folder, Letter to Charles Profitt, October 11, 1968).

A decade later, beginning in 1953, Frank Tannenbaum was one of the featured speakers at the 22nd Annual Governor's Conference on "Youth and Community Service," sponsored by the state of Illinois. The invitation to speak originated from none other than Clifford R. Shaw, director of the Chicago Area Project. At this conference, Frank's presentation was titled "Education for Crime," which closely followed Chapter 3 in *Crime and the Community*. At the same conference, Tannenbaum (1953b) gave another presentation titled "The Place for the Offender," in which he reiterated many of his historic positions. First, there are no good penal institutions. "The effect of the institution is to make the criminal less competent to return to a normal community and be as he was before he was sent away" (p. 49). In answer to a question as to whether we can abolish the penitentiary, Tannenbaum answered, "[N]o, obviously, because there is probably no alternative. But we can reduce the role of the penal institution within our world." In this regard, Tannenbaum endorsed efforts to avoid first arrests on juveniles, the use of probation, the expanded use of fines, and a distinction drawn between the professional criminal and the accidental offender. "I would take the drug addict, for instance, and treat him as a sick man, not as a criminal" (p. 50). He even endorsed the regulation of certain illegal behaviors of the time, referring specifically to the amount of criminality created by Prohibition. As to the residue of men left in the prison system, Tannenbaum again pointed to the work of his mentor, Thomas Mott Osborne. He recommended the creation of "convict communities" within the prison walls, with their own constitution, executive, and judicial system.

> The experiment didn't last long because of political interference, but the influence of Osborne on American penal institutions was very great. For eight or ten years, I attended an annual diner given for Thomas Mott Osborne by the men who had been discharged from Sing-Sing and in kinds of crimes and who had long criminal careers, but something had happened to them in

CRIME AND THE COMMUNITY

this process, and they weren't ashamed of the fact that they had been in prison. They testified at this dinner not of their past criminal careers but of their present membership in an ordinary community.

(p. 52)

Finally, Tannenbaum warned his audience that it "will require a great deal of charity and understanding on the part of the outside community to accept the fact that this man has been washed clean—that he's not a 'different' human being" (p. 53)

Frank's presentation titled "Education for Crime" was later published in 1954. It reiterated his work in *Crime and the Community*. Tannenbaum described gang formation as largely random activity by boys who are longing for companionship, love, and support. But in the course of these often-noisy, mischievous activities, others in the neighborhood begin to label the young boys as "trouble makers." However, if something is stolen or suddenly broken, the police are called. Now, one or more of the boys are arrested, and a labeling process starts. For youngsters with more than one arrest or who are accused of serious felonies, the possibility of a commitment to a youth reformatory looms. Observes Tannenbaum (1954: 10):

You send him to an institution because you look over the place and say that the mother and father aren't competent to take care of him. The home isn't too good. The neighborhood is bad. If you send him to an institution for three months, or six months, he will, you think, come back a reformed boy. Something useful will happen to him.

But according to Tannenbaum, "there are no good institutions." The "more efficient an institution is, the worse it is." When the reformatory lad returns to the community, his time "upstate" becomes a badge of honor. He has learned more sophisticated ways of living on the street from other, often older inmates at reform school. When something happens in the neighborhood, boys with a prior record are the first to be detained and questioned. Upstanding members of the community have now decided that this lad and his gang friends are common criminals. In this cybernetic process (Tannenbaum, 1954:11):

Then something else has happened. This boy gradually, with your help, converts himself and identifies himself as a criminal.

95

The point I am trying to make is that we quite unconsciously compel a very young boy to choose a career, and in this case, it is that of a professional criminal.

Tannenbaum went on to criticize the entire criminal justice system as failing to reform the delinquents they process. He argued that individualized treatment was "a false path," because in a majority of cases, it fails. Instead, Tannenbaum suggested that the system be geared to not making that initial arrest, and instead work with a delinquent group in the community and use local resources to shape behavior. As one can readily see, Tannenbaum was endorsing alternatives to labeling, which later became nonintervention (Schur, 1973) and the early design of what became known as the detached gang worker model (Klein, 1965).

Frank Tannenbaum married the former Jane Belo, an anthropologist and specialist on Southeast Asia, on May 22, 1940 (Marrero, 2013). Miss Belo came from a wealthy Texas family (newspapers), and she met Frank through famed Columbia University anthropologist Margaret Mead. This would be her third marriage. Shortly thereafter, Jane Belo Tannenbaum purchased a farm near the town of Peekskill in Putnam County, New York. It would become known as Canopus Hollow Farm and was a favorite resting spot of the Tannenbaums. The pair also traveled extensively in Central and South America. Jane had finished her B.S. in anthropology at Columbia and worked on a doctorate from Columbia, circa 1946–1949, but never finished (Marrero, 2013: 28). Unfortunately, Jane Tannenbaum likely suffered from bipolar disorder as well as alcoholism. During the last decade of her life, she was often

Figure 8.2 A young Jane Belo before her marriage to Frank Tannenbaum in 1940

CRIME AND THE COMMUNITY

hospitalized. She passed away on April 3, 1968, after a long illness (*New York Times,* obituaries, April 4, 1968, p. 47) and was buried near the Tannenbaum family farm in Putnam Valley, New York. At her request, an endowment of approximately $1.5 million dollars was donated to the Columbia University Seminar program.

9

FRANK'S CONTRIBUTION TO CONVICT CRIMINOLOGY

As to why Frank Tannenbaum discontinued any further research into the subject of criminology, perhaps a quote from a letter he wrote to Hans W. Mattick on November 5, 1964, will suffice (Tannenbaum Collection, Box 31). At the time, Mattick (1965) was attempting to solicit an updated article from Frank on his thoughts about prisons.

> I tried to explain to Father Taylor last spring that I have not done any writing about crime or prisons since I published my *Crime and the Community* which was a long time ago. I have completely lost touch with the problem and have during the last thirty years been involved in Mexico, Latin America, labor and political theory and unfortunately I am one of those people who cannot write at all unless he is deeply involved emotionally and psychologically.

In a 1956 letter to a student inquiring as to his early interest in criminology, Frank replied that "[i]n my own case, criminology has been a side issue and a hobby, and my original interest in it derives from the fact that I spent a year in prison (Box 8, Folder E, Letter to Bruce Eckland, dated January 9, 1956). Nevertheless, as illustrated by this very monograph, Frank Tannenbaum's early career in criminology was more than just a passing "hobby."

Frank Tannenbaum has been described by criminologist Imogene Moyer (2001) as a nontraditional voice in American criminology. Indeed, his contributions to labeling theory, the group process in delinquency, the origins of professional crime, and the concept of the dramatization of evil remain historically important to the field.

But it was his role as a convict criminologist and critic of the American penal industry that remains largely unrecognized. Tannenbaum used his personal experiences in the American gulag to become a leading reformer of prisons and an academic who wrote on the subject with a sense of outrage. It is regretful that neither the punishment industry nor its allied academicians have bothered to resurrect his critique of the entire system. With high levels of imprisonment still dominant in America, we are experiencing the sad results of this failed experiment (Pattillo, Weiman, & Western, 2004). In fact, it is one theme of this monograph that Tannenbaum's critique, informed by his convict status, remains largely valid to this day.

That Tannenbaum did not continue to write about criminology is partly due to his long-time interest in the politics of Mexico and Latin America. Beginning in the 1920s, Tannenbaum started publishing both books and articles on Latin America, and his interest in criminology naturally waned.

Nevertheless, when a researcher asked Frank about his experience at Blackwell's Island prison in 1914–1915, he had this remembrance [Box 6, Folder B(3), Letter of November 29, 1962 to W. David Lewis]:

> I suppose I ought to say to you that prisons are peculiarly ingrown institutions. The best of prisons in time generate a situation which often ends in riot and disturbance. It is not just the physical condition of the prison that matters most. It is the psychological environment within which men live day in and day out that in the end precipitates the kind of reaction that makes the public ask for an investigation.

Indeed, when contacted by convict author Alfred Hassler (1954) for commentary on Hassler's book, *The Diary of a Self-Made Convict*, Tannenbaum wrote: "You have written a true and deeply moving book. The American prison is as you describe it" (Box 9, Folder H (1), Letter to A. Hassler dated January 19, 1954). Hassler had written of his experiences as a conscientious objector when confined to Lewisburg Federal Penitentiary. Harry Elmer Barnes (1954) would later write the foreword to Hassler's monograph.

In an unpublished draft titled "Man and His Institutions," Tannenbaum (1957) observed that "something like two-thirds of the inmates in penal institutions are recidivists" (Box 35, Institutions Folder, n.d.). Despite the ostensible purpose of prisons to deter inmates from returning, Frank argued that "one way of [ensuring] that a man will continue to go to prison is to send him there in the first place." The very nature of the institutions, in Tannenbaum's view, sets up a "psychological expectancy" on the part of both the prison and its inmates, "which tends to be fulfilled."

> Upon his release he joins friends made in the prison, and finds occupation among men who have careers similar to his own, and in time, he returns to prisons. And he, his friends, his keepers, and the police expect him to return and do another "stretch."
>
> What we have is a character molded, shaped, and identified as a prison type . . . It needs merely to be added that "good" prisons and "bad" prisons have an essentially similar influence upon their inmates . . . [A]s long as it stands committed to the role it plays in our society—that of keeping the body of the convicted criminal—it cannot escape its own logic.

One issue that may represent a failing on the part of Frank Tannenbaum was his abandonment of a class analysis of prisons and their function in American society (Rusche & Kirchheimer, 1939; Taylor, Walton, & Young, 1993; Quinney, 2000; Shelden, 2001; Davis, 2003, 2005; Western, 2006; Reiman, 2007). Starting out as a young anarchist with ties to none other than Emma Goldman, Tannenbaum slowly abandoned this perspective and his radical associates for a more liberal analysis of society. To quote labor radical Elizabeth Gurley Flynn (1955: 169):

> He was sentenced to a year on Blackwell's Island and $500 fine, with the proviso that if the fine was not paid the sentence was to be increased by another year and a half. He served the year, the fine was paid and that ended the labor career of Frank Tannenbaum. Some philanthropic-minded people aided him to complete his education and he ultimately became a professor at Columbia University, where he now is. The poor and lowly remained with us.

A survey of Jewish radicals from the 1880s to the late 1920s does not even mention Frank Tannenbaum (Michels, 2012). Some 19 books on this very subject failed to even mention Frank's 1914 arrest and subsequent imprisonment (Michels, 2012: 333). In fact, towards the end of his remarkable career, Tannenbaum adopted a kind of conservative pluralism that never explained either the creation of the penitentiary in America or why it continued to function despite its many failings. One can only speculate as to why Tannenbaum abandoned an anarchist perspective on prisons and criminology. During the time he entered

Columbia University as an undergraduate, the U.S. Department of Justice had jailed many Industrial Workers of the World (IWW) leaders beginning in 1917, and later inaugurated the famous Palmer raids (1920) in which at least 10,000 so-called leftists were arrested, deported, or prosecuted under various espionage and sedition acts (Avrich, 1995; Murray, 1955; Stone, 2004). Tannenbaum was clearly on the list of former IWW supporters, but his previous imprisonment and the Palmer raids may have convinced him to abandon risky thinking.

He expressed his philosophy quite distinctly in a 1952 report by the Advertising Council on the subject of civil liberties (Box 22, Advertising Council Folder, Report of Round Table dated May 26, 1952, pp. 6–7):

> Mr. Tannenbaum evinced his satisfaction that "so much of the effective political power in our society" was lodged in the local community. He pointed out that no President of the United States can be assured of a docile Congress because the Congress is dependent upon local political machines, not upon the President, for election—as in the long run, is the President himself. He understood "freedom" to mean "responsibility," and he was bothered by the "drift in the United States" toward a centralization of powers at Washington. He stood for the parish first, then the township, then the county, the state, the Federal Government.
>
> The last-named was the weakest of the lot; the first-named the strongest. The trend in the nation seemed to him to be to take responsibility for the family away from the family and place it in the state—this in the name of some ideal—efficiency, for instance—but surely of a mistaken ideal. He preferred local inefficiencies to efficiency that came from a great distance. "If," he said, "we are going to preserve American democracy in the long run, and if we are not to have a centralized state," this trend must be reversed.

Tannenbaum was quite hostile to classic Marxist analysis, especially what he called Russian communism, which he associated with concentration camps (Box 1, Correspondence with Lazaro Cardenas, February 24, 1956). As previously stated, he was critical of economic interpretations of society, which included William's (1944) *Capitalism and Slavery* and even the work of C. Wright Mills (Tannenbaum, 1946; Papers, Box 23, Anaconda Company file, Letter to C. Brinckerhoff, December 7, 1960).

Instead, Tannenbaum veered more to what labor scholar Michael Merrill (Winn, 2010: 110) has described as "closer to Veblen than Marx." In a letter to a nun Tannenbaum summarized his political orientation this way (Box 12, Folder M(4) Letter to Sister Gertrudis Musi, dated January 13, 1967):

> I am not a socialist and I don't believe I have ever been one. I am more nearly a Jeffersonian democrat, if that means anything to you, and in rebellion against the effects of industrialization upon the individual and society. In desperation, this has made me into a believer in trade unionism and a species of syndicalism. This is not my first choice, but it is a way of protecting the individual against the impersonality of the machine.

Hence, he argued that "American industrial and economic development is tied up with the absence of class structure" (Box 22, Advertising Council, Round Table , Discussion, June 23, 1952, p. 4) Toward the end of his career, Tannenbaum even defended the United States against charges of imperialism and oppression to his colleagues in Latin America, making this argument in *The American Tradition in Foreign Policy* (1955).[1] In 1966, he joined a statement defending the U.S. military's presence in South Vietnam as a means of fighting communism (Box 35, Freedom House file, correspondence to H. Gideonse, dated 1966). In private correspondence, Tannenbaum defended the American intervention in Guatemala to overthrow the Jacobo Arbenz regime (Box 15, Folder S(2), letter to Jesus Scarpetta dated December 6, 1955). In addition, he insisted that his analysis of the labor movement in *A Philosophy of Labor* (1951) was non-Marxist (Box 15, Folder S(2), Letter to Harry Stark, dated May 25, 1954). Toward the very end of his illustrious career, Frank (1968) even extolled the virtues of the multinational corporation as a replacement for the failed nation-state and the United Nations.

It is no surprise then that several observers have labeled Tannenbaum's views on society as fundamentally conservative (Rossiter, 1955; Viereck, 2006). Even one of his best friends, who wrote an introduction to *The Balance of Power in Society*, characterized Frank as "profoundly conservative" (Randall, 1969).[2] Thus, Philip Foner (1965: 448) notes that Tannenbaum played a minor role in the IWW after his arrest and imprisonment, later becoming a professor at Columbia University "specializing in labor relations, Latin America, and anti-radicalism."

But on subject of crime and prisons, Tannenbaum never wavered, and his own views could hardly be described as conservative. He was opposed to the architecture of the American penitentiary and thought that most offenders ought not to be incarcerated. Tannenbaum opposed capital punishment and was a member of the American League to Abolish Capital Punishment (Box 28, committee membership folder, letter of May 20, 1940, from Vivian Pierce). He believed that prisons ought to emphasize educational habitation, the principles of Osborne's Mutual Welfare League, and re-entry (parole) into society. When asked his opinion about progress in penology in March 1950, Tannenbaum had this to say:

Q. *Are you denying the possibility of progress in penology and anything else?*

TANNENBAUM: You'd have to ask if the aims of society are better accomplished now by prisons or in the 18th century. I think there's been no progress, or little (Box 46, Transcript for Philosophy 236, Progress File).

He was an early labeling theorist and argued that the very process of arresting and incarcerating delinquents produced the recidivist, and that the psychological and physical terror of the penitentiary was a complete and utter failure—if judged by reducing recidivism. The late Donald Cressey pointed out that Tannenbaum was likely the first American criminologist to address the labeling effect, with the help of two famous "symbolic interactionists": John Dewey and Thorsten Veblen. Robert King Merton (1948) took up Tannenbaum's analysis in his "self-fulfilling prophecy," and so did Edwin Lemert in 1951 (Cressey, 1965).

In 1965, Hans Mattick (1965: 8) would even describe Frank as one of the three most respected living penologists, next to Thorsten Sellin and Harry Elmer Barnes, who represented more than 100 years of study and research on prison problems.

Frank Tannenbaum's own experience of imprisonment and habilitation may provide some direction to the very issue of re-entry now plaguing the American prison industry. Upon his release from prison in 1915, Frank became the beneficiary of a private stipend to attend Columbia University. He graduated from Columbia in 1921, and it was that experience—in effect, a retooling of a young, working-class immigrant—that enabled him to escape the "convict" label and shield him from a return to the penitentiary as a recidivist. Here, the data are very clear that intensive educational and vocational training programs for convicts do reduce criminal reprocessing (Taylor, 1992; Jacobson, 2005; Piché, 2008). Unfortunately, Frank's own experience

Figure 9.1 One of Frank's favorite photographs, relaxing at the cottage

was contrary to the principle of "less eligibility" that has characterized imprisonment throughout the world.

The recent emergence of the convict criminology movement may owe some debt to Frank Tannenbaum, who has been described "as the first convict criminologist" (Belknap, 2015: 8). Convict criminology is the study of crime and its institutions from the standpoint of convicts who have personally experienced the criminal justice system and have chosen to write authoritatively about the subject. Many of these convicts have gone on to obtain advanced degrees and even teach at colleges and universities (Ross & Richards, 2003). Frank Tannenbaum was clearly a trailblazer, producing a body of work heavily influenced by his own experience in the American gulag over 100 years ago. As we resurrect his long-forgotten contributions to the field, what remains fascinating is how many of his observations remain quite relevant even today.

Of tangential interest, Frank Tannenbaum was a victim of a robbery in 1966, in which he was slashed with a knife by one of the two assailants (*New York Times*, June 29, 1966; Gaulkin, 1966). The incident resulted in a huge outpouring of cards, telegrams, and letters from all over the world. Both suspects were later arrested, but only one was convicted and sentenced to Elmira Reformatory.

Tannenbaum passed away from cancer on June 1, 1969—the 25th anniversary of the Columbia University Seminars. His legacy in North American criminology is celebrated in this book.

Notes

1 See letter to Jose Pages Llergo, dated March 27, 1962, Box 15, Siempre Folder. This letter concerned various anti-American speeches given by intellectuals in Mexico during a 1962 conference in which Frank gave a presentation on the ideological bases of international relations in the Americas.
2 In the John Herman Randall papers at Columbia University, Professor Randall actually described his friend Frank as "profoundly conservative, or, more accurately, reactionary—his Utopia is Stone Age culture" (Box 18, Randall papers, Tannenbaum manuscript).

APPENDIX

New York Law Journal

September 24, 2014 Wednesday
SECTION: COURT DECISIONS; Pg. p. 22, col.5 Vol. 252 No. 59
LENGTH: 756 words
HEADLINE: IN THE MATTER of THE ADOPTION of CHILDREN WHOSE FIRST NAMES ARE ZALKIND AND SARA File Nos.: 77X 1931 and 78X 1931;
DECISIONS;
First Judicial Department;
Bronx County;
SURROGATE'S COURT
BYLINE: Surrogate Malave-Gonzalez
COURT: Surrogate's Court, Bronx County
IN THE MATTER of THE ADOPTION of CHILDREN WHOSE FIRST NAMES ARE ZALKIND AND SARA File Nos.: 77X 1931 and 78X 1931—This is an application by an academician, a "criminologist," for access to records contained in sealed adoption files that he avers will be useful to him in connection with a biography that he is writing about the adoptees' alleged biological father. Notarized statements are filed from the adoptee's alleged daughter and the fiduciary of the estate of an alleged brother of the biological father that they do not object to unsealing these records. The petitioner notes that the adoptions predate the 1938 enactment of DRL §114 (2) and contends that these files now constitute archival records for which the general purposes of DRL 114 (2) no longer apply and, "given the public interest aspects of the application, the instant petition should not be separately sealed as it comes from a third party source, none of the materials are confidential, and these pleadings belong in the "public domain."

APPENDIX

In New York State, the sealing of adoption records has been mandated since 1938, but courts have had discretionary power to seal such records since 1924. Adoption records remain sealed pursuant to DRL §114 to protect confidentiality "which is vital to the adoption process" to provide anonymity to the natural parents, enable the adoptive parents to form a close bond with their adopted child, protect the adopted child from possibly disturbing information that might be found in his records, and allow the state to foster an orderly and supervised adoption system (see Matter of Linda F. M. 52 NY2d at 236 [1981], appeal dismissed 454 US 806 [1981]; Matter of Candy, M.M.M. (38 Mise 3d 1228 [A]; 2013 NY Slip Op 50312 [U] [Sur Ct, Nassau County 2013]; Matter of Hayden, 106 Mise 2d [Sup Ct, Albany County 1981]).

Nonetheless, adoption records may be unsealed pursuant to DRL §114 (2), usually for medical grounds, upon the application of the adoptee or the adoptive parents, after a showing of "good cause" accompanied by a certification from a physician licensed to practice medicine in New York State that the records are required to address a serious physical or mental illness, upon due notice to the adoptive parents and to such additional persons as the court may direct (see Matter of Peter B., 12 Mise 3d 1184 [A] [Sur Ct, Nassau County 2006]). Good cause has been found for non medical reasons, such as to establish Hungarian lineage for purposes of citizenship (see Matter of Victor M. I. II., NYLJ, Mar. 30, 2009, at 25, col 1 [Sur Ct, Nassau County 2009]), apply for Turkish citizenship after a close relationship was established with the birth mother (see Matter of S. P., NYLJ, May 13, 2010, at 38, col 3 [Sur Ct, Bronx County 2010]), or to establish membership in the Hopi Tribe (see Matter of Merri H. F., NYLJ, May 27, 2005, at 5, col 1 [Sur Ct, Kings County 2005]).

No good cause warranting unsealing was found for the following purposes: to establish Puerto Rican heritage in order to participate in a basketball draft (see Matter of C. C., NYLJ, Jan. 7, 2010 at 40, col4 [Sur Ct, Kings County 201 0], learn the identities of biological relatives (see Matter of Linda F. M. 52 NY2d at 240), make the adoptee aware of a biological brother (see Matter of Robert R. B., 147 Mise 2d 569 [Fam Ct., Schoharie County 1990]), or ascertain the birth mother's religion (see Matter of Alica L. L. T. (38 Mise 3d 966 [Sur Ct, Nassau County 2012]).

In weighing the request for disclosure against the privacy interests at stake, the petitioner must spell out a "concrete and compelling need that is credibly connected to the adoptee's lack of knowledge of his parentage (see Matter of Theodore, NYLJ, June 15, 2012, at 22, col 4 [Sur Ct, New York County 2012]). No such compelling reasons exist here. The petitioner is not a party to the adoption or related to the adoptive or biological relatives, and his stated purpose is to obtain information concerning the biological father for publication in the father's biography. That the adoption records are old do not support unsealing. Otherwise, the statute's requirement of good cause would become a nullity and adoption records could be unsealed after the mere passage of time (see Matter of R. S., NYLJ, Oct. 25, 2006, at 32, col 1 [Sur Ct, Kings County 2006]).

Accordingly, the application is denied. The Chief Clerk shall mail a copy of this decision, which constitutes the order of the court, to the petitioner.

September 18, 2014

APPENDIX

To be argued by: Adam Paskoff, Esq
(Time Requested: 8 minutes)

SUPREME COURT OF THE STATE OF NEW YORK
APPELLATE DIVISION - FIRST DEPARTMENT

IN THE MATTER OF THE ADOPTION OF
CHILDREN WHOSE FIRST NAMES ARE

ZALKIND AND SARA

Docket No(s).:
77X-1931
and
78X-1931

BRIEF IN SUPPORT OF PETITIONER-APPELLANT

Adam Paskoff, Esq.
Paskoff & Tamber, LLP
Attorneys for Appellant,
MATTHEW G. YEAGER, PH.D.
225 W. 34th Street, Suite 1303
New York, N.Y. 10122
Tel: (212) 643-5454
Fax: (212) 643-2346
Email: skofflaw@gmail.com

APPENDIX

TABLE OF CONTENTS

Page

TABLE OF AUTHORITIES ii

PRELIMINARY STATEMENT 1

QUESTIONS PRESENTED ON APPEAL 3

STATEMENT OF RELEVANT FACTS 4

    THE PETITION 6

    THE DECISION BELOW 6

ARGUMENTS:

    I. THE ADOPTION RECORDS IN QUESTION PREDATE MANDATORY SEALING AND NO ORDER SEALING SUCH RECORDS ARE KNOWN TO EXIST, THEREBY RENDERING THE REQUESTED RECORDS PUBLIC RECORDS CONSISTENT WITH THE TREATMENT OF ADOPTION RECORDS AT THAT TIME 7

    II. ALTERNATIVELY, UNDER THE UNIQUE FACTS PRESENTED HEREIN, GOOD CAUSE HAS BEEN ESTABLISHED TO UNSEAL THIS ADOPTION RECORD 9

CONCLUSION 15

CERTIFICATION PURSUANT TO 22 NYCRR § 670.10.3(F) 16

STATEMENT PUSUANT TO CPLR 5531 17

AFFIRMATION OF SERVICE 19

APPENDIX

TABLE OF AUTHORITIES

CASES

In re Adoption of G., 906 N.Y.S.2d 488, 489 (Sur Ct, Bronx County 2010)..........12

Golan v. Louise Wise Services, 514 N.Y.S.2d 682 (1987) 12

Matter of Alicia L. L. T., 38 Misc.3d 966 [Sue Ct, Nassau County 2012])............10

Matter of Candy, M.M.M. (38 Misc.3d 1228(A); 2013 N.Y. Slip Op. 50312 [U](Sur Ct, Nassau County 2013 8

Matter of C. C., NYLJ, Jan. 7, 2010, col 4 [Sur Ct, Kings County 2010]) 10

Matter of Hayden, 106 Misc.2d (Sup Ct, Albany County 1981)..............................9

Matter of Linda F. M. 52 N.Y.2d at 236 (1981), appeal dismissed 454 U.S. 806 (1981) 8, 10, 11, 13

Matter of Linda J. W., 682 N.Y.S.2d 565 (Family Court, Genesee County 1998).14

Matter of Merri H. F., NYLJ, May 27, 2005, at 5, col 1 [Sur Ct, Kings County 2005]) 10

Matter of Robert R. B., 147 Misc.2d 569 [Fam Ct, Schoharie County 1990]) 10

Matter of R. S., NYLJ, Oct. 25, 2006, at 32, col 1 [Sur Ct, Kings County 2006]) .10

Matter of S. P., NYLJ, May 13, 2010, at 38, col 3 [Sur Ct, Bronx County 2010])...9

Matter of Victor M. I. II., NYLJ, Mar. 30, 2009, at 25, col 1 [Sur Ct, Nassau County 2009]) 9

STATUTES

DRL §114.. 1, 3, 6, 7, 8, 9, 11, 13, 17

OTHER

Block, Inciardi & Hollowell, Historical approaches to crime: research strategies and issues (Beverly Hills, California: Sage, 1977)..14

111

APPENDIX

Hibbert, The roots of evil: a social history of crime and punishment (Boston: Little Brown, 1963) 14

Renne, The search for criminal man: a conceptual history of the dangerous offender (Lexington, Mass: Lexington Books, 1978) 14

Elizabeth J. Samuels, "The Idea of Adoption: An Inquiry into the History of Adoptee Access to Birth Records," 53 Rutgers L. Rev. 367 (2001) 8

Matthew G. Yeager, Ph.D., "Frank Tannenbaum: The Making of a Convict Criminologist", The Prison Journal 91 (June 2011): 177-197, No. 2.......................4

APPENDIX

PRELIMINARY STATEMENT

This appeal addresses the legal issues involved in a request to review an adoption record from 1931; or, alternatively, an application to unseal said adoption record based upon a showing of good cause, which was denied by the Surrogate's Court of the State of New York, County of Bronx (Malave-Gonzalez, Surr.) in a decision and order dated September 18, 2014. The records are sought by an academician for research related to the birth father, Frank Tannenbaum, a historical figure. All of the parties to the adoption are now deceased, and consent has been given by the surviving relatives to the Estate of Frank Tannenbaum (birth father) and the Estate of Zalkind Hurwitz (adopted son). Surrogate Malave-Gonzalez did not address the legal argument that this adoption predates Domestic Relations Law ("DRL") § 114, which was enacted in 1938, requiring all adoption records subsequent thereto to be sealed. There is no known order sealing the requested records, thereby making the record in question public consistent with the availability of such files back in 1931.

Alternatively, appellant seeks reversal of the court's decision denying the unsealing of the adoption record and argues that "good cause" has been established as required by DRL § 114(2). The request is made by a non-party to the adoption, Matthew G. Yeager, Ph.D., Associate Professor of Criminology, Department of Sociology, King's University College, Western University, Canada, for research

113

APPENDIX

purposes. The within appeal is an issue of first impression in the State of New York with grave impact upon establishing standards in determining "good cause" in similar situations, pursuant to a term not defined by statute.

While the entire adoption record was sought by the applicant, alternatively, he requested the date that both children were adopted, their dates of birth, their legal adoptive names and the names and dates of birth of the adoptive parents. Further, the applicant requested the ability to review, but not copy said record.

APPENDIX

Questions Presented On Appeal

1. Whether, in the absence of an Order sealing the record, is there a statutory bar to the release of Court records from 1931;

2. Whether it was proper to consider granting access to a 1931 adoption record under the statutory requirements of a subsequent law (DRL § 114(2)) enacted in 1938; and

3. Alternatively, whether the applicant, an academician, has established good cause pursuant to DRL § 114(2) for purposes of research where there is virtually no negative impact to any family members, where the principal parties of the divorce are now deceased, where surviving family members have consented to the release of such information, and where the release of such records materially assist in the research of an historical figure.

APPENDIX

STATEMENT OF RELEVANT FACTS

The applicant, Matthew G. Yeager, Ph.D., is writing a biography on Frank Tannenbaum, expanding upon an article entitled "Frank Tannenbaum: The Making of a Convict Criminologist" published in The Prison Journal 91 (June 2011): 177-197, No. 2. [RA at 23]. Mr. Tannenbaum is a historical figure, who is an early American convict criminologist noted for his depiction of the dramatization of evil, which was an early precursor to the later developed labeling theory. The biography would not be complete without an analysis of his personal life discussing the subject's social history, accurate facts, and humanization that allows the reader into the life of the subject. As stated by Professor Yeager, "this request goes beyond mere curiosity" because "[o]ne's social history becomes part of the historical record in a biography." [RA at 16].

All the relevant participants to the adoption are now deceased. Frank Tannenbaum (birth father), was born March 4, 1883 in Galacia, Austria, and emigrated to the United States in 1905. He died in Manhattan on June 1, 1969. On June 1, 1917, Frank married Esther Abramson (birth mother) in the Bronx. [RA at 40]. Esther was born in New York City on June 2, 1895 [RA at 42] and died, upon information and belief, on August 30, 1957. Public Health Records for the City of New York indicate that Frank and Esther had a son named Zalkind born in Manhattan on November 4, 1925. [RA at 44].

APPENDIX

Frank and Esther divorced in Sonora, Mexico in 1929. The divorce papers reveal that there was a daughter born to this union, upon information and belief, on June 29, 1927. After the divorce, Esther remarried Eli Hurwitz in or about 1929. Records indicate that they had two children, Zalkind Hurwitz and Saranessa Hurwitz (a/k/a Saralneus Hurwitz). The family resided in Brooklyn and were also known by the last name Hurowitz [RA at 46].

The JewishGen Burial Registry and death certificate reveal that a Zalkind Hurwitz, with the same birth date above, passed away in Florida on June 23, 1994 [RA at 48 and 50]. Information furnished to the applicant through the surviving daughter of Zalkind Hurwitz indicates that Nessa Hurwitz Sternfeld passed away on May 18, 2011, in Tarrytown, New York. [RA at 53].

The Social Security Death Index reveals that the adoptive father, Eliahu Hurwitz, died in July of 1968, most likely in the Bronx, New York [RA at 51]. Thus all parties directly related to this adoption proceeding are now deceased.

Consenting to the release of the records is Frank's surviving nephew, Sherman W. Tanenbaum, the sole legal heir to the Estate of Frank Tanenbaum. [RA at 67 and 69]. Also consenting to the release of the records is Annette Hurwitz Jenner, daughter of Zalkind Hurwitz. [RA at 66 and 70].

APPENDIX

The Petition

Professor Yeager, a criminologist of more than 42 years, requested access to the Tannenbaum adoption in connection with his detailed research into Frank Tannenbaum's life for purposes of completing his biography on the subject. A detailed factual record was set forth in the Surrogate's Court with a request for access to the adoption file on the basis of two theories, to wit: 1) The adoption, which was completed in 1931, was not sealed and predated the automatic sealing requirements of DRL § 114, which was enacted in 1938., thereby making said adoption records a public record consistent with such records of that time; and, alternatively, 2) an application was made based upon a showing of good cause pursuant to DRL § 114(2).

The Decision Below

The Honorable Nelida Malave-Gonzalez, Surrogate, Bronx County, denied the request to access the adoption records in a written decision dated September 18, 2014 [RA at 8]. Surrogate Malave-Gonzalez analyzed the application solely under a theory of unsealing for good cause pursuant to the standards required in DRL § 114(2), determining that no compelling reason exists in weighing disclosure against the privacy interests at stake. There was no detailed analysis weighing the privacy issues protected by DRL § 114 against an academic request for research which has no negative impact on the same.

APPENDIX

Arguments

I.

THE ADOPTION RECORDS IN QUESTION PREDATE MANDATORY SEALING AND NO ORDER SEALING SUCH RECORDS ARE KNOWN TO EXIST, THEREBY RENDERING THE REQUESTED RECORDS PUBLIC RECORDS CONSISTENT WITH THE TREATMENT OF ADOPTION RECORDS AT THAT TIME

The adoption in question concluded in 1931. DRL § 114 was not enacted until 1938. Surrogate Malave-Gonzalez did not directly address this argument, but in a circuitous way referenced that courts had the discretionary power to seal adoption records since 1924. There is no reference by the Court of an existing Order sealing the adoption record in question. Based on the record before this Appellate Division there is no basis to seal this adoption record 84 years after-the-fact. If the Judge or Surrogate presiding over the adoption in 1931, with full knowledge of the discretionary right to seal such record, chose not to do so, then there can be no justifiable reason for the record to be sealed 84 years later.

Surrogate Malave-Gonzalez stated no reason to treat this adoption record as sealed. The Surrogate did state that the function of sealing an adoption record was "to protect confidentiality 'which is vital to the adoption process' to provide anonymity to the natural parents, enable the adoptive parents to form a close bond with their adopted child, protect the adopted child from possibly disturbing information that might be

APPENDIX

found in his records, and allow the state to foster an orderly and supervised adoption system" citing cases from 1981 and 2013[1]. All of the stated reasons are valid and important to adoptions made pursuant to DRL § 114, but none of the reasoning is applicable to the adoption that is the subject of this matter.

All of the principals to this adoption are now deceased, and there is no basis to seal this adoption record 84 years after-the-fact when neither the biological parents, adoptive parents, or adopted children are alive to reap the benefit of confidentiality, and the purpose of allowing a close bond to form between the adoptive parents and adopted children. As further discussed herein, the rational behind sealing the record is inapplicable to this matter, which was an adoption presumably done on consent, with the biological mother remaining the parent and only her second husband adopting the children. On that basis, there is no need for anonymity of the natural parents.

Historically, adoption records were publicly available in the 1920's and 1930's. *See* Elizabeth J. Samuels, "The Idea of Adoption: An Inquiry into the History of Adoptee Access to Birth Records," 53 Rutgers L. Rev. 367 (2001). Inasmuch as there is no evidence that this record was sealed based on discretion of the presiding Judge or Surrogate prior to 1938, this adoption file is a matter of public record and should be released to Professor Yeager.

---

1 Surrogate Malave-Gonzalez cited Matter of Linda F. M. 52 N.Y.2d at 236 (1981), appeal dismissed 454 U.S. 806 (1981); Matter of Candy, M.M.M. (38 Misc.3d 1228(A); 2013 N.Y. Slip Op. 50312 [U](Sur Ct, Nassau County

APPENDIX

II.

ALTERNATIVELY, UNDER THE UNIQUE FACTS PRESENTED HEREIN, GOOD CAUSE HAS BEEN ESTABLISHED TO <u>UNSEAL THIS ADOPTION RECORD</u>

Surrogate Malave-Gonzalez went through a perfunctory analysis of unsealing

the record pursuant to the standards set forth in DRL § 114(2), which states in relevant

part:

> No person, including the attorney for the adoptive parents shall disclose the surname of the child directly or indirectly to the adoptive parents except upon order of the court. No person shall be allowed access to such sealed records and order and any index thereof except upon an order of a judge or surrogate of the court in which the order was made or of a justice of the supreme court. No order for disclosure or access and inspection shall be granted except on good cause shown and on due notice to the adoptive parents and to such additional persons as the court may direct.

The statute is silent as to what constitutes good cause. Although not specified by

the statute, both the petitioner and the Court recognize that the most common basis to

establish a showing of good cause is usually for medical grounds. However, Courts

have found good cause for non-medical reasons, with the Surrogate Court citing

examples of establishing Hungarian lineage for purposes of citizenship (Matter of

Victor M. I. II., NYLJ, Mar. 30, 2009, at 25, col 1 [Sur Ct, Nassau County 2009]);

apply for Turkish citizenship after a close relationship was established with the birth

mother (Matter of S. P., NYLJ, May 13, 2010, at 38, col 3 [Sur Ct, Bronx County

---

2013); Matter of Hayden, 106 Misc.2d (Sup Ct, Albany County 1981).

APPENDIX

2010]); or to establish membership in the Hopi Tribe (Matter of Merri H. F., NYLJ, May 27, 2005, at 5, col 1 [Sur Ct, Kings County 2005]).

Surrogate Malave-Gonzalez cited examples where other courts did not find good cause to establish Puerto Rican heritage in order to participate in a basketball draft (Matter of C. C., NYLJ, Jan. 7, 2010, col 4 [Sur Ct, Kings County 2010]); learn the identities of biological relatives (Matter of Linda F. M., 52 N.Y.2d at 240); make the adoptee aware of a biological brother (Matter of Robert R. B., 147 Misc.2d 569 [Fam Ct, Schoharie County 1990]); or ascertain the birth mother's religion (Matter of Alicia L. L. T., 38 Misc.3d 966 [Sue Ct, Nassau County 2012]).

What is clear is the application by Professor Yeager, an academician, is an issue of first impression. Surrogate Malave-Gonzalez concluded "[t]hat the adoption records are old do not support unsealing. Otherwise, the statute's requirement of good cause would become a nullity and adoption records could be unsealed after the mere passage of time" citing Matter of R. S., NYLJ, Oct. 25, 2006, at 32, col 1 [Sur Ct, Kings County 2006]). While petitioner does not argue that the aforesaid reasoning is incorrect, it is respectfully argued that the passage of time should be a factor considered among all other factors in determining whether good cause is established. To disregard the passage of time entirely does a disservice to the purpose of sealing records in protecting the anonymity of parties and allowing the adoptive parents to

APPENDIX

form a close bond with the adopted child.

None of the examples cited by the Court either for or against unsealing an adoption record relate to the facts of this matter which is for purposes of academic research. No one is arguing that academic research by itself should trump the confidentiality of a recent adoption matter that properly involves the protections afforded by DRL § 114. However, in the case at bar, the protections do not apply, and Surrogate Malave-Gonzalez has issued a Decision and Order that essentially states that academic research can never be a basis to unseal adoption records. There is no statutory bar to an application to unseal adoption records for historical research related to the biological father. It is respectfully submitted, that such conclusion renders the requirement of assessing "good cause" a nullity as the facts of this particular application were never considered. This conclusion is contrary to the case relied on by the Court, In re Matter of Linda F. M., 52 N.Y.2d 236, 240 (1981), appeal dismissed, 454 U.S. (1981)("By its very nature, good cause admits of no universal black-letter definition. Whether it exists, and the extent of disclosure that is appropriate, must remain for the courts to decide on the facts of each case.").

Surrogate Malave-Gonzales did not invoke a balancing test and consider relevant factors such as 1) the degree of the need for disclosure; 2) the wishes of the adoptive and biological parents; and 3) the potential effects upon both set of parents

APPENDIX

and their families. *See* Golan v. Louise Wise Services, 514 N.Y.S.2d 682 (1987). Had the balancing test been considered, all of the factors support unsealing of this record. Where non-medical information is sought, courts in New York have held that access will be granted "where the person seeking the information makes a request, if granted, will benefit the petitioner and will not have an adverse impact on the interests of the adopted child or the adoptive or biological parents." In re Adoption of G., 906 N.Y.S.2d 488, 489 (Sur Ct, Bronx County 2010).

In this matter, Professor Yeager has set forth, in detail, the historical relevance of the biological father. The background history and circumstances surrounding the adoption are relevant to the chronology of his personal life. The information sought is consistent with background information gathered by researchers in biographies in general. Every single basis cited by the Surrogate's Court in denying the request to unseal the adoption record is now irrelevant to the adoption in question:

1. Anonymity to the natural parents – The only adoptive parent was the adoptive father. The natural parents, adoptive father, and adopted children are all deceased. Representatives of the estates of the parties involved are all aware of the adoption and consent to the release of the records. Further, it appears that this adoption was made upon consent of the birth father, thereby rendering anonymity between the parties as moot.

2. Enable the adoptive parents to form a close bond with the adoptive child – Since the relevant parties are now deceased, the unsealing of this adoption record will not impact that intent in the least.

3. Protect the adopted child from possibly disturbing information that might be

APPENDIX

found in his records – Both adopted children are deceased. An in camera inspection can be made for any "disturbing information", which is unlikely since the mother's second husband adopted the children and the facts of this adoption are known by the surviving family members.

4. Allow the state to foster an orderly and supervised adoption system – Release of this record will not impact on the orderly nature of the adoption system since the adoption in question was completed 84 years ago. DRL § 114 remains in place for all adoptions subsequent to 1938.

Having addressed the public policy of sealing records, we will now address the

arguments in favor of good cause proffered by Professor Yeager.

The applicant is a criminologist with 42 years experience and a Professor at

King's College, Western University, Canada. [RA at 32]. In 2013-2014, the applicant

was a visiting scholar at the Department of Sociology, Columbia University, working

with archival documents maintained by Columbia related to the subject, Frank

Tannenbaum. Frank Tannenbaum is a subject of historical relevance in the field of

sociology and criminology, and was the subject of an earlier 2011 article by Professor

Yeager. [RA at 23].

Good Cause must rise above a desire to learn one's identity or mere curiosity.

See In re Matter of Linda F. M. v. Dept. of Health, City of New York, 437 N.Y.S.2d

283, *cert. denied*, 454 U.S. 806 (1981). Professor Yeager set forth his need for this

information because "[t]he importance of a historical figure, like Frank Tannenbaum,

is not just his contributions to the field of criminology, but includes a chronology of his

APPENDIX

personal life.... These aspects of a subject's social history provide context, accurate facts, humanization, and allow for the telling of a story that interests the reader." [RA at 16]. Therefore, the request goes beyond mere curiosity and as discussed above, has no negative impact on the parties to the adoption proceeding.

Professor Yeager further argued to the Surrogate's Court that:

> Historical research in criminology and sociology has, over the years, produced a large body of important findings about the origins of criminological thought. See Block, Inciardi & Hollowell, **Historical approaches to crime: research strategies and issues** (Beverly Hills, California: Sage, 1977). Cf. Renne, **The search for criminal man: a conceptual history of the dangerous offender** (Lexington, Mass: Lexington Books, 1978); Hibbert, **The roots of evil: a social history of crime and punishment** (Boston: Little Brown, 1963). These historical contributions represent public good, and are often written in the public interest. It is respectfully submitted that "good cause" as a concept incorporates both the public good and public interest.

[RA at 16].

Precedence exists granting the application to unseal adoption records by a third-party unrelated to the adoption. *See* Matter of Linda J. W., 682 N.Y.S.2d 565 (Family Court, Genesee County 1998)(Unsealing granted to the Clear Sky Band of the Onondaga Indian Nation for purposes of determining whether an adoptee was a member of an Indian tribe and qualified for benefits under the Indian Child Welfare Act). Therefore, Professor Yeager has standing to make this application, respectfully, submitting it is in advancement of the public good and without any negative impact on the parties to this adoption.

APPENDIX

CONCLUSION

For the foregoing reasons it is respectfully requested that Professor Yeager's

petition to release the 1931 adoption records be granted.

Dated: New York, New York
April 23, 2015

Respectfully Submitted,
PASKOFF & TAMBER, LLP

ADAM PASKOFF
Attorneys for Appellant
MATTHEW G. YEAGER, PH.D.
225 W. 34th Street, Suite 1303
New York, NY 10122
(212) 643-5454

APPENDIX

CERTIFICATE OF COMPLIANCE PURSUANT TO
22 NYCRR § 670.10.3(f)

The forgoing brief was prepared on a computer. A proportionally spaced typeface was used, as follows:

        Name of Typeface: Times New Roman
        Point Size: 14
        Line Spacing: Double

The total number of words in the Brief, inclusive of point headings and footnotes and exclusive of pages containing the table of contents, table of citations, proof of service, certificate of compliance, or any authorized addendum containing statutes, rules, regulations, etc., is 3,242.

APPENDIX

SUPREME COURT OF THE STATE OF NEW YORK
APPELLATE DIVISION - FIRST DEPARTMENT
—————————————————————————————————X
IN THE MATTER OF THE ADOPTION OF,
CHILDREN WHOSE FIRST NAMES ARE

ZALKIND and SARA

Docket No(s).: 77X-1931 and 78X-1931

—————————————————————————————————X

STATEMENT PURSUANT TO CPLR 5531

1.   The Docket Numbers in the Surrogate's Court were Docket nos.: 77X-1931 and 78X-1931.

2.   The full names of the parties are set forth in the caption above. There have been no changes.

3.   The action was commenced in the Surrogate's Court, Bronx County on May 27, 2014.

4.   No notice was required because all parties requiring notice are deceased and the Surrogate's Court did not direct any further notice be served.

5.   The object of the action is a motion to review adoption records from 1931, which predated the statute that requires mandatory sealing of adoption records; or alternatively a motion to unseal adoption records based upon a showing of good cause pursuant to Domestic Relations Law § 114(2).

129

APPENDIX

6.   The appeal is from a decision and order of the Surrogate's Court, Bronx County dated September 18, 2014, denying the request to review the adoption file and denying the request to unseal adoption records on the basis of good cause

7.   The appeal is on the appendix method.

APPENDIX

SUPREME COURT OF THE STATE OF NEW YORK
APPELLATE DIVISION - FIRST DEPARTMENT
————————————————————————X

IN THE MATTER OF THE ADOPTION OF,
CHILDREN WHOSE FIRST NAMES ARE

ZALKIND and SARA

Docket No(s).: 77X-1931 and 78X-1931

————————————————————————X

AFFIRMATION OF SERVICE

ADAM PASKOFF, an attorney at law for the State of New York, hereby

affirms upon penalties of perjury being duly sworn, deposes and says that:

This was an application to unseal adoption records in the Surrogate's Court, State of
New York, County of Bronx. No party requiring notice is still alive. The Court did not
direct any other party to be served Notice. Therefore, this Record of Appeal is not
being served on any other party.

Dated: April 23, 2015

_____
ADAM PASKOFF

REFERENCES

Alexander, Michelle (2010) *The New Jim Crow: Mass Incarceration in the Age of Colorblindness.* New York: The New Press.

Anderson, Frank V. (1921) "Labor Movement as Seen By an ex-I.W.W. College Graduate" *New York Tribune* July 3, 1921, p. 8.

Arciniegas, German (1970) "Tannenbaum and Latin America" *Americas* 22(4): 27–31.

Associated Press (October 24, 1931) "Wickersham Report Is Called Too Mild" *Miami Herald*, p. 17.

Avrich, Paul (1995) *Anarchist Voices: An Oral History of Anarchism in America.* Princeton, NJ: Princeton University Press.

Bain, Read (1938) "Review of *Crime and the Community.*" *American Sociological Review* 3(3): 414–416.

Baker, Newman F. (1935) "Prison Notes" *Journal of Criminal Law & Criminology* 25(6): 957–96.

Barnes, Harry Elmer (1926) *The Repression of Crime.* New York: G. H. Doran.

Barnes, Harry Elmer (1954) Foreword to Alfred Hassler's *Diary of a Self-Made Convict.* Chicago: H. Regnery Co.

Bayonne Times (January 5, 1935) "Tannenbaum to Return to Scene of Early Studies—as Professor," p. 8.

Becker, Howard S. (1963) *Outsider: Studies in the Sociology of Deviance.* New York: Free Press.

Belknap, Joanne (2015) "Activist Criminology: Criminologists' Responsibility to Advocate for Social and Legal Justice." *Criminology* 53(1): 1–22.

Bennett, James V. (1935) "American Prisons—Houses of Idleness" *The Survey* 71(4): 99–101.

Berkman, Alexander (1910) "The Need of Translating Ideals into Life" *Mother Earth* 5(9): 292–296.

Breit, Harvey (March 11, 1951) "Talk with Frank Tannenbaum" *New York Times Book Review*, p. 10.

Brommel, Bernard J. (1978) *Eugene V. Debs: Spokesperson for Labor and Socialism.* Chicago, IL: Kerr Publishing.

Cantor, N. (1934) "Book Review of *Osborne of Sing Sing.*" *Annals of the American Academy of Political and Social Sciences* 173: 221.

REFERENCES

Carson, E. Ann (2014) "Prisoners in 2013." Washington, D.C.: Bureau of Justice Statistics, U.S. Department of Justice, September, NCJ 247282.

Chamberlain, Rudolph W. (1935) *There Is no Truce: A Life of Thomas Mott Osborne.* New York: The Macmillan Company.

Chambliss, William J. (1973) "The Saints and the Roughnecks" *Society* 11(1): 24–31.

Chapman, John Jay (1927a) "Thomas Mott Osborne," *Harvard Graduates' Magazine* 35(139): 465–476.

Chapman, John Jay (1927b) "Osborne's Place in Historic Criminology" *Harvard Graduates' Magazine* 35(140): 599–605.

Christie, Nils (2000) *Crime Control as Industry* (3rd ed.). London: Routledge.

Clayton, Jr., Obie (ed.) (1996) *An American Dilemma Revisited: Race Relations in a Changing World.* New York: Russell Sage Foundation.

Cook, Charles (1891) *The Prisons of the World: With Stories of Crime, Criminals and Convicts.* London: Morgan and Scott.

Cressey, Donald R. (1965) , "Use of Criminals in Rehabilitation" in *Key Issues: A Journal of Controversial Issues in Criminology,* edited by Hans Mattick. Chicago, IL: St. Leonard's House, vol. 2, pp. 96–97.

Cullen, Frances T. and Pamela Wilcox (eds.) (2010) *Encyclopedia of Criminological Theory,* Los Angeles, CA: Sage Publications, vols. 1 & 2.

Current Opinion (1921) "The Labor Movement as Seen by a Former Mob Leader," 71(3): 342–344.

Davis, Angela Y. (2003) *Are Prisons Obsolete?* New York: Seven Stories Press.

Davis, Angela Y. (2005) *Abolition Democracy: Beyond Empire, Prisons, and Torture.* New York: Seven Stories Press.

Dell, Floyd (1927). *Upton Sinclair: A Study in Social Protest.* London: Doran & Co.

Delpar, Helen (1988) "Frank Tannenbaum: The Making of a Mexicanist, 1914–1933" *The Americas* 45(October): 153–171.

Dunlap, Richard (August 18, 1929) "Prison System Is Criticized at Virginia Forum" *New York Tribune*, p. 18.

Durose, Matthew, Cooper, Alexia and Snyder, Howard (2014) "Recidivism of Prisoners Released in 30 States in 2005: Patterns from 2005 to 2010" Washington, D.C.,: Bureau of Justice Statistics, U.S. Department of Justice, April, NCJ 244205.

Eastman, Max (1914a) "The Church and the Unemployed" *The Masses* 5(7): 10–11.

Eastman, Max (1914b) "The Tannenbaum Crime" *The Masses* 5(36): 6–8.

Eastman, Max (likely author) (1914c) "The Catholic Church and the Unemployed" *International Socialist Review* 14(April): 608–609.

Eastman, Max (1955) *Reflections on the Failure of Socialism.* New York: Devin-Adair.

Ellis, Havelock (1910) *The Criminal.* (4th ed.) London: W. Scott Pub. Company.

Falk, Candice (ed.) (2003) *Emma Goldman: A Documentary History of the American Years.* Berkeley, CA: University of California, Berkeley Press, vols. 1–3).

Federal Bureau of Investigation. U.S. Department of Justice. (2008) File on Frank Tannenbaum under FOIPA No. 1117024–000. Washington, D.C. September 17.

Feld, Rose C. (July 8, 1934) "Osborne in Triumph and Defeat" *New York Times Book Review*, p. 6.

Field, Anne P. L. (1915) *The Story of Canada Blackie.* New York: E. P. Dutton & Company.

Flynn, Elizabeth Gurley (1955) *I Speak My Own Piece: Autobiography of "The Rebel Girl."* New York: Masses & Mainstream.

REFERENCES

Flynn, Frank T. (1950) "The Federal Government and the Prison-Labor Problem in the States. II. The Prison Industries Reorganization Administration" *Social Service Review* 24(2): 213–236.

Folsom, Franklin (1991) *Impatient Armies of the Poor: The Story of Collective Action by the Unemployed, 1808–1942.* Boulder, CO: University Press of Colorado.

Foner, Philip S. (1965) *Industrial Workers of the World.* History of the Labor Movement in the United States (New York: International Publishers, Volume 4).

Fowler, Dorothy G. (1981) *A City Church: The First Presbyterian Church in the City of New York, 1716–1976.* New York: First Presbyterian Church.

Friedman, Lawrence M. (1993) *Crime and Punishment in American History.* New York: Basic Books.

Gaulkin, Charles (June 28, 1966) "Chances Good for Stabbed Columbia Prof" *New York Post,* p. 2.

Gertzman, Jay A. (2013) *Samuel Roth, Infamous Modernist.* Gainsville, FL: University of Florida Press.

Glaze, Lauren and Danielle Kaeble (2014) "Correctional Populations in the United States, 2013," Washington, D.C.: Bureau of Justice Statistics, U.S. Dept. of Justice, December, NCJ 248479.

Glazer, Nathan (1961) *The Social Basis of American Communism.* New York: Harcourt, Brace and World, pp. 28–29, 95.

Goldman, Emma (1931) *Living My Life.* New York: Alfred A. Knopf, vol. 2.

Gordon, Mary L. (1922) *Prison Discipline.* New York: E. P. Dutton.

Hale, Charles A. (1995) " Frank Tannenbaum and the Mexican Revolution" *Hispanic American Historical Review* 75(2): 215–246.

Harris, Leon (1975) *Upton Sinclair: American Rebel.* New York: Thomas Crowell Co.

Hassler, Alfred (1954) *The Diary of a Self-Made Convict.* Chicago, IL: H. Regnery Co.

Headen, T.P. (April 24, 1937) "1914 Originator of Sit-down Is Soft-Spoken Scholar Now" *New York Sun,* p. 4.

Healy, William (1915) *The Individual Delinquent: A Text-book of Diagnosis and Prognosis for all Concerned in Understanding Offenders.* Boston, MA: Little, Brown & Co.

Hirsch, Adam Jay (1992) *The Rise of the Penitentiary: Prisons and Punishments in Early America.* New Haven, CT: Yale University Press.

Hirschhorn, Bernard (1997) *Democracy Reformed: Richard Spencer Childs and His Fight for Better Government.* Westport, CT: Greenwood Press.

Holmes, John Haynes (1914) "Tannenbaum in the Large," *The Survey Magazine* 32(4): 94–95.

In the Matter of the Adoption of Children Whose First Names Are Zalkind and Sara (2014). Surrogate's Court for Bronx County, State of New York, Case Nos. 77X-1931 and 78X-1931. *New York Law Journal* 252(59)" col. 5, p. 22. See appendix.

Jacobson, Michael (2005) *Downsizing Prisons: How to Reduce Crime and End Mass Incarceration.* New York: New York University Press.

Jacoby, Joseph E. (1979) *Classics of Criminology.* Oak Park, IL: Moore Publishing, pp. 192–193.

Jacoby, Joseph E., Theresa Severance and Alan S. Bruce (2012) *Classics of Criminology.* (4th ed.) Long Grove, IL: Waveland Press, chapter 41.

REFERENCES

Jaquith, L. Paul (1973) "The University Seminars at Columbia University: A Living Monument to Frank Tannenbaum." New York: Unpublished Ph.D. dissertation in education, Columbia University.

Jennings, Al (1921) *Through the Shadows with O. Henry.* New York: H. K. Fly Company.

Johnson, Robert and Hans Toch (eds.) (1982) *The Pains of Imprisonment.* Beverly Hills, CA: Sage Publications.

Jones, Thai (2012) *More Powerful than Dynamite: Radicals, Plutocrats, Progressives, and New York's Year of Anarchy.* New York: Walker & Company.

Kirchheimer, Otto (1938) "Book Review of *Crime and the Community*" *Zeitschrift für Sozialforschung* 7: 466.

Kleiman, Mark, Angela Hawken, and Ross Halperin (March 18, 2015) "We don't need to keep criminals in prison to punish them." VOX Media. Retrieved from: www.vox.com/2015/3/18/8226957/prison-reform-graduated-reentry.

Klein, Malcom W. (1965) "Juvenile Gangs, Police, and Detached Workers: Controversies about Intervention," *Social Service Review* 39: 183–190.

Kyckelhahn, Tracey (2015) "Justice Expenditure and Employment Extracts, 2012—Preliminary." Washington, D.C.: Bureau of Justice Statistics, U.S. Department of Justice, NCJ 248628, February 26, 2015, Table 1.

Leary, John J., Jr. (March 3, 1917) "Wade and Hurd Open Prison Reform" *New York Tribune*, p. 8.

Leary, John J., Jr. (March 4, 1917) "Transferred Inmates Tell of Clinton Brutalities" *New York Tribune*, Part I, p. 10.

Lemert, Edwin M. (1951) *Social Pathology: A Systematic Approach to the Theory of Sociopathic Behavior.* New York: McGraw-Hill.

Lohman, Joseph D. (1939) "Book Review of *Crime and the Community*." *American Journal of Sociology* 45(2): 280–281.

Lombroso, Cesare (1911) *Crime, Its Causes and Remedies.* Boston, MA: Little, Brown & Company.

Lombroso-Ferrero, Gina (1911) *Criminal Man* (according to the classification of Cesare Lombroso, briefly summarized by his daughter Gina Lombroso-Ferrero). New York: Putnam.

Lowrie, Donald. (1912) *My Life in Prison.* New York: John Lane.

Luhan, Mabel Dodge (1936) *Intimate Memories: Movers and Shakers.* New York: Harcourt, Brace and Company, vol. 3.

Maier, Joseph and Richard Weatherhead (1974) *Frank Tannenbaum: A Biographical Essay.* New York: Columbia University.

Maier, Joseph and Richard Weatherhead (1974) "Introduction to Tannenbaum" in *The Future of Democracy in Latin America.* New York: Alfred A. Knopf.

Maik, Thomas A. (1994) *The Masses Magazine (1911–1917).* New York: Garland Publishing.

Marrero, Georgina (2013) "Bali in Her Soul: A Portrait of Jane Belo." New York: Columbia University Seminar on the History of Columbia, Nov. 6, 2013, draft manuscript. Office of Columbia University Seminars.

Masses, The (1914) "Tannenbaum's Speech," 8 (May): 3, No.36.

Masses, The (1915) "And Frank Tannenbaum" 6 (February): 9, No. 5. [documents change in municipal housing and policing in NYC following Tannenbaum's trial and imprisonment].

REFERENCES

Masses, The (1915) "Katherine B. Davis' Little Hell" 6 (September): 20, No. 12. [documents result of investigation by State Commission on Prisons, indicting Blackwell's Island and calling for retirement of warden].

Mattick, Hans W. (1965) (ed.) *Key Issues: A Journal of Controversial Issues in Criminology.* Chicago, IL: St. Leonard's House, vol. 2.

Matza, David (1969) *Becoming Deviant.* Englewood Cliffs, NJ: Prentice-Hall.

McCole, John, Seyla Benhabib, and Wolfgang BonB (1993) "Max Horkheimer: Between Philosophy and Social Science" in S. Benhabib, W. BonB, and J. McCole (eds.) *On Max Horkheimer.* Cambridge, MA: MIT Press.

McLennan, Rebecca M. (2008) *The Crisis of Imprisonment: Protest, Politics, and the Making of the American Penal State, 1776–1941.* New York: Cambridge University Press.

McNair, John Frederick A. (1899) *Prisoners Their Own Warders.* Westminster, UK: A. Constable & Company.

Merton, Robert K. (1948) "The Self Fulfilling Prophecy," *Antioch Review* 8(2): 195.

Meyer, Charles H. Z. (1939) "Crime a Group Project," *Federal Probation* 3(3): 38.

Michels, Tony (2012) *Jewish Radicals: A Documentary History.* New York: New York University Press.

Moyer, I. L. (2001) *Criminological Theories: Traditional and Non-Traditional Voices and Themes* (Thousand Oaks, CA: Sage).

Murphy, Kevin P. (2008) *Political Manhood: Red Bloods, Mollycoddles & the Politics of Progressive Era Reform.* New York: Columbia University Press.

Murray, Robert K. (1955) *Red Scare: A Study in National Hysteria, 1919-1920* (Minneapolis, MN: University of Minnesota Press).

Murton, Thomas O. (1976) *The Dilemma of Prison Reform.* New York: Holt, Rinehart and Winston.

Murton, Thomas O. and J. Hyams (1969) *Accomplices to the Crime: The Arkansas Prison Scandal.* New York: Grove Press.

Myrdal, Gunnar (1944) *American Dilemma: The Negro Problem and Modern Democracy.* New York: Harper & Brothers.

National Recovery Administration (1934) *Report of Committee on Competition of Products of Cotton Garment Industry with Products of Prison Labor as Directed by Executive Order No. 118–135.* Washington, D.C.: November 26, 1934.

Nelson, Victor Folke (1933) *Prison Days and Nights.* Boston, MA: Little, Brown & Co.

New York Call (1914a) "Army of Jobless Arrested After it is Denied Shelter at St. Alphonsus Church" March 5, 1914, pp. 1–2, 6.

New York Call (1914b) "Socialists to Open Fight for Jobless" March 6, 1914, pp. 1–2.

New York Call (1914c) "Unemployed Meet in Square Despite Inclement Weather" March 7, 1914, pp. 1–2.

New York Call (1914d) Editorial. March 12, 1914, p. 6.

New York Call (1914e) "Lawyers' Wrangles Mark Opening of Tannenbaum Trial" March 25, 1914, p. 3.

New York Call (1914f) "Prosecution Rests Unexpectedly in Tannenbaum Trial" March 26, 1914, p. 3.

New York Call (1914g) "Reporters Spring Sensations at the Tannenbaum Trial" March 27, 1914, p. 1–2.

New York Call (1914h) "Tannenbaum Guilty Is Jury's Verdict" March 28, 1914, pp. 1–2.

New York Call (1915) "Osborne Tells of Prison Work" April 18, 1915, p. 2.

REFERENCES

New York Sun (1915) "Tannenbaum Welcome Decorous as Tea Party," March 10, 1915, p. 14.

New York Times (1914a) "I.W.W. Invaders Seized in Church." March 5, 1914, p. 1.

New York Times (1914b) "Police Drive I.W.W. Crowd from Park" March 6, 1914, pp. 1, 3.

New York Times (1914c) "Anarchists Spread Alarm in 5th Ave." March 22, 1914, p. 1.

New York Times (1914d) "Says I.W.W. Leader Expected Violence," March 25, 1914, p. 6.

New York Times (1914e) "I.W.W. Mob Forced Church Door Lock," March 26, 1914, p. 5.

New York Times (1914f) "Tannenbaum's Men Testify for Him," March 27, 1914, p. 7.

New York Times (1914g) "Tannenbaum Guilty Gets a Year in Jail," March 28, 1914, p. 1.

New York Times (1914h) "Quiet on Island; Miss Davis There," July 11, 1914, pp. 1, 3.

New York Times (1914i) "Tannenbaum Tamed by Hunger, Gives Up," July 14, 1914, p. 5.

New York Times (1914j) "Tannenbaum Still in Cell," July 15, 1914, p. 18.

New York Times (1915) "Tannenbaum Set Free," March 10, 2015, p. 6.

New York Times (1915) "Spirit Prisoner from I.W.W. Meet" March 14, 1915, Part 11, p. 10.

New York Times (1915) "Osborne Criticises Blackwell's Island" April 18, 1915, Part II, p. 15.

New York Times (1915) "Militia to Quell Bayonne Rioters; 1 Dead, Many Hurt" July 22, 1915, pp. 1,4.

New York Times (1915) "IWW Bomb Meant for Rockefeller Kills Four of Its Makers, Wrecks Tenement and Injures Many Tenants," July 5, 1914, pp. 1–2.

New York Times (1915) "Strikers Control Bayonne; Fielder Balks at Troops" July 24, 1915, p. 5.

New York Times (1915) "Sheriff's Nerve Ends Oil Strike" July 28, 1915, pp, 1, 4.

New York Times (1915) "Kinkaid Arrests 99 Strike Guards" July 29, 1915, p. 18.

New York Times (1917) ""I.W.W. Now Crop Up in New Guide" December 1, 1917, p. 3.

New York Times (1921) "Tannenbaum Wins Academic Honors" June 5, 1921, p. 19.

New York Times (1931) "Prisons of Nation Declared Failure; Outworn, Inhuman," July 27, 1931, pp. 1, 4.

New York Times (1931) "Penologists Back Wickersham Data," October 23, 1931, p. 17.

New York Times (1966) "Slashed Professor Identifies Suspects", June 29, 1966, p. 14.

New York Tribune (1915) "Tannenbaum may return to College," March 11, 1915, p. 4.

New York Tribune (1915) "No job, no rent! Slogan Sounded by Tannenbaum" March 14, 1915, p. 9.

O'Hare, Kate Richard (1923) *In Prison.* New York: A.A. Knopf.

Orth, Samuel P. (1919) *The Armies of Labor.* New Haven, CT: Yale University Press.

Osborne, Thomas Mott (1914) *Within Prison Walls.* New York: Appleton Company, republished by Patterson Smith Publishing, Montclair, NJ, 1969.

Osborne, Thomas Mott (1916) *Society and Prisons: Some Suggestions for a New Penology.* New Haven: Yale University Press, republished by Patterson Smith Publishing, Montclair, NJ, 1975.

Osborne, Thomas Mott (1922) "Introduction" in *Wall Shadows: A Study in American Prisons.* New York: G. P. Putnam's Sons, pp. v–xii.

Osborne, Thomas Mott (1924) *Prisons and Common Sense.* Philadelphia, PA: J. B. Lippincott Company.

Pattillo, Mary, David Weiman and Bruce Westerns (eds.) (2004) *Imprisoning America: The Social Effects of Mass Incarceration.* New York: Russell Sage Foundation.

Perkins, Frances (1955) "Reminiscences of Frances Perkins: Oral History." Transcripts. Columbia University. Butler Library.

REFERENCES

Piché, Justin (2008) "Education in Prisons—Special Issue" *Journal of Prisoners on Prisons* 17(1).

Potter, Ellen C. (1934) "Book Review of *Osborne of Sing Sing*," *Social Science Review* 8(3): 554–556.

Prison Association of New York (1916) "The New Day in Prison Reform."(Albany, NY: J. B. Lyon Printers, Parts I & II, 71th annual report for 1915.

Putnam, George Palmer (June 26, 1921) "The New Tannenbaum" *New York Times* Section 6—Amusements, p. 3.

Quinney, Richard (2000) *Bearing Witness to Crime and Social Justice.* Albany, NY: State University of New York Press, chapters 5 and 7.

Randall, Jr., John Herman (1969) "Introduction" in *The Balance of Power in Society and Other Essays.* New York: MacMillan Company.

Reiman, Jeffrey (2007) *The Rich Get Richer and the Poor Get Prison.* (8th ed.) Boston, MA: Allyn & Bacon.

Robinson, Arthur (1925) "Rebels in Retirement," *Collier's* 75(2): 17–18.

Roosevelt, Franklin D., Presidential Library, Hyde Park, New York. Official file 459 "Prisons."

Ross, Jeffrey Ian and Stephen Richards (2003) *Convict Criminology.* Belmont, CA: Wadsworth.

Ross, Stanley R. (1970) "Obituary, Frank Tannenbaum," *Hispanic-American Historical Review* 50(2): 345–348.

Rossiter, Clinton (1955) *Conservatism in America.* New York: Alfred A. Knopf, pp. 261–262.

Rothman, David J. (1980) *Conscience and Convenience: The Asylum and Its Alternatives in Progressive America.* Boston, MA: Little, Brown and Company.

Roulston, Jane A. (1914) "The I. W. W. and Events in New York," *Solidarity* 5(239): 1, 4.

Rusche, Georg and Otto Kirchheimer (1939) *Punishment and Social Structure.* New York: Columbia University Press.

Saposs, David J. (1926) *Left Wing Unionism.* New York: International Publishers.

Schulman, Harry (1938) "Review of *Crime and the Community*," *National Lawyers Guild Quarterly* 1(4): 346–348.

Schur, Edwin M. (1973) *Radical Non-Intervention: Rethinking the Delinquency Problem.* Englewood Cliffs, NJ: Prentice-Hall.

Schwendinger, Herman and Julia Schwendinger (1970) "Defenders of Order or Guardians of Human Rights?" *Issues in Criminology* 5(2): 123–157.

Sellin, Thorsten (1944) *Pioneers in Penology.* Philadelphia, PA: University of Pennsylvania Press.

Sellin, Thorsten (1976) *Slavery and the Penal System.* New York: Elsevier Scientific Publishing Company.

Shaw, Clifford R. and Henry D. McKay (1931) "Social Factors in Juvenile Delinquency," *Report on the Causes of Crime.* Washington, D.C.: Government Printing Office, vol. 11, no. 13, Wickersham Commission.

Shelden, Randall G. (2001) *Controlling the Dangerous Classes.* Boston, MA: Allyn & Bacon.

Shoham, Shlomo and G. Rahav (1968) "Current Survey Research and Methodology, Social Stigma and Prostitution," *British Journal of Criminology* 8(4): 402–412.

Stone, G. R. (2004) *Perilous Times: Free Speech in Wartime from the Sedition Act of 1978 to the War on Terrorism* (New York: Norton).

REFERENCES

Survey, The (March 28, 1914) "The Churches, the City, and the 'Army of the Unemployed' in New York" 31(26): 792–795.

Sutherland, Edwin H. (1924) *Criminology.* Philadelphia, PA: J. B. Lippincott.

Tannenbaum, Frank (1914) "Tannenbaum's Speech," *The Masses* 5(8): 2.

Tannenbaum, Frank (1915) "Prison Literature," *The Masses* 6(7): 6.

Tannenbaum, Frank (1915a) "What I Saw in Prison," *The Masses* 6(8): 8–9.

Tannenbaum, Frank (1915b) "The Blackwell's Island Hell," *The Masses* 6(9): 16–17.

Tannenbaum, Frank (1915c) "A Strike in Prison," *The Masses* 6(10): 16–18.

Tannenbaum, Frank (1916) "Book Review of Osborne's *Within Prison's Walls,*" *The Masses* 8(4): 19.

Tannenbaum, Frank (1916) "Blackwell's Revisited," *The Masses* 8(6): 24.

Tannenbaum, Frank (1919a) "Life in an Army Training Camp," *The Dial* April 5, pp. 3–12.

Tannenbaum, Frank (1919b) "Tannenbaum Not 'Reformed,'" *New York Call* December 23, p. 8.

Tannenbaum, Frank (1920) "Prison Cruelty," *Atlantic Monthly* 125 (April): 433–444.

Tannenbaum, Frank (1920) "Prison Democracy," *Atlantic Monthly* 126(4): 433–434.

Tannenbaum, Frank (ed.) (1920) *The Six-Hour Shift and Industrial Efficiency.* New York: Henry Holt & Co.

Tannenbaum, Frank (1921a) "A Radical at Columbia," *New York Times,* July 12, p. 12.

Tannenbaum, Frank (1921b) "Prison Facts," *Atlantic Monthly* 128(5): 577–588.

Tannenbaum, Frank (1921c) *The Labor Movement: Its Conservative Functions and Social Consequences.* New York: G. P. Putnam's Sons.

Tannenbaum, Frank (1922a) "Facing the Prison Problem," *Atlantic Monthly* 129: 207–217.

Tannenbaum, Frank (1922b) *Wall Shadows: A Study in American Prisons.* New York: G. P. Putnam's Sons.

Tannenbaum, Frank (1922c) "The Most Helpless," *The Churchman* 125–126: 12–14.

Tannenbaum, Frank (1923) "The Ku Klux Klan," *Century Magazine* 105(6): 873–882.

Tannenbaum, Frank (1923a) "Southern Prisons," *Century Magazine* 106(3): 387–398.

Tannenbaum, Frank (1923b) "The Miracle School," *Century Magazine* 106(4): 499–506.

Tannenbaum, Frank (1924) *Darker Phases of the South.* New York: Putnam.

Tannenbaum, Frank (1924b) "The Career of Crime," *The Standard [New York: American Ethical Union]* 11(3): 87–90.

Tannenbaum, Frank (1924c) "Prisoners and Prisons," *The Standard [New York American Ethical Union]* 11(4): 124–125.

Tannenbaum, Frank (1925) "The Professional Criminal: An Inquiry into the Making of Criminals," *Century Magazine* 110(5): 577–588.

Tannenbaum, Frank (1930a) "The Vision that Came to Thomas Mott Osborne," *The Survey Magazine* 65(1): 7–11, 52–53, 55.

Tannenbaum, Frank (1930b) "When Osborne Came to Sing Sing," *The Survey Magazine* 65(3): 156–158, 182–182, 189, 192.

Tannenbaum, Frank (1930c) "The Community that Osborne Built," *The Survey Magazine* 65(5): 266–270, 301, 303–304.

Tannenbaum, Frank (1931a) "Osborne under Fire," *The Survey Magazine* 65(7): 378–381, 399–401.

Tannenbaum, Frank (1931b) "The Ordeal of Thomas Mott Osborne," *The Survey Magazine* 65(11): 614–616, 623–625.

REFERENCES

Tannenbaum, Frank (1933) *Osborne of Sing Sing*. Chapel Hill, NC: University of North Carolina Press.

Tannenbaum, Frank (1938) *Crime and the Community*. Boston, MA: Ginn & Company.

Tannenbaum, Frank (1940) "Address of Dr. Frank Tannenbaum before the Annual Meeting of the National Committee on Prisons and Prison Labor," May 2, 1940. New York City, reprint [Box 54, Tannenbaum Papers].

Tannenbaum, Frank (1943) "Forward" in *New Horizons in Criminology*. New York: Prentice-Hall, Inc. pp. v–viii.

Tannenbaum, Frank (1944) "An American Dilemma," *Political Science Quarterly* 58(3): 321–340.

Tannenbaum, Frank (1946) *Slave and Citizen: The Negro in the Americas* (New York: Knopf).

Tannenbaum, Frank (1946) "A Note on the Economic Interpretation of History," *Political Science Quarterly* 61(2): 247–253.

Tannenbaum, Frank (1946) "The Balance of Power in Society," *Political Science Quarterly* 61(4): 481–504.

Tannenbaum, Frank (1951) *A Philosophy of Labor*. New York: Knopf.

Tannenbaum, Frank (1953a) "The University Seminar Movement at Columbia University," *Political Science Quarterly* 68(2): 161–180.

Tannenbaum, Frank (1953b) "The Place for the Offender," in *Proceedings, 22nd Annual Governor's Conference on Youth and Community Service*. Chicago, IL: Illinois Youth Commission, pp. 49–53.

Tannenbaum, Frank (1954) "Education for Crime," **Public Aid in Illinois** 21(7): 8–13.

Tannenbaum, Frank (1955) *The American Tradition in Foreign Policy*. Norman, OK: University of Oklahoma Press.

Tannenbaum, Frank (1957) "Man and His Institutions" in *La Miscelanea de Estudios Dedicados a Dr. Fernando Ortiz*. Havana, Cuba, vol. III, pp. 1409–1416.

Tannenbaum, Frank (ed.) (1965) *A Community of Scholars: The University Seminars at Columbia*. New York: Praeger.

Tannenbaum, Frank (1968) "The Survival of the Fittest," *Columbia Journal of World Business* 3(2): 13–20, 17.

Tannenbaum, Frank (1969) *The Balance of Power in Society and Other Essays*. New York: MacMillan Company, chapter 15.

Tannenbaum, Frank (1974) *The Future of Democracy in Latin America*. New York: Alfred A. Knopf. See pp. 3–45 for biographical essay.

Taylor, Ian, Paul Walton, and Jock Young (1973) *The New Criminology*. London: Routledge & Kegan Paul.

Taylor, Jon Marc (1992) "Post-Secondary Correctional Education: Evaluation of Effectiveness and Efficiency," *Journal of Correctional Education* 43(3): 132–141.

Thrasher, Frederic M. (1927) *The Gang,* Chicago, IL: University of Chicago Press.

Trooboff, Peter D. (December 15, 1961) "Phi Beta, But …," *Columbia Spectator*, p. 3.

Ureles, Sonia (March 10, 1915) "Jail Term Over, He Tells of It," *The Call,* p. 3.

Viereck, Peter (2006) *Conservative Thinkers: From John Adams to Winston Churchill*. (2 ed.) New Brunswick, NJ: Transaction Publishers, pp. 100–101.

Vold, George B. (1938) "Review of *Crime and the Community*," *Annals of the American Academy of Political and Social Science* 198(1): 242.

Vold, George B. (1952) "Review of *Crime and the Community*," *Journal of Criminal Law, Criminology & Police Science* 43(1): 86–88.

REFERENCES

Vorse, Mary Heaton (1935) *A Footnote to Folly: Reminiscences of Mary Heaton Vorse.* New York: Farrar & Rinehart.

Washington Post (1931) "Tannenbaum Hits System of Prisons," October 23, p. 4.

Western, Bruce (2006) *Punishment and Inequality in America.* New York: Russell Sage Foundation.

Winn, Peter (2010) "Frank Tannenbaum Reconsidered: Introduction," *International Labor and Working-Class History* 77 (Summer): 109–114.

Whitfield, Stephen J. (2013) "Out of Anarchism and into the Academy," *Journal for the Study of Radicalism* 7(2): 93–124.

Wickersham Commission Reports. (1931) No. 9 *Report on Penal Institutions, Probation and Parole.* Washington, D.C.: U.S. Government Printing Office.

Williams, Eric E. (1944) *Capitalism & Slavery.* Chapel Hill, NC: University of North Carolina Press.

Wisotsky, Isidore (1978) Papers. "Such a Life" unpublished manuscript. Taminent Library and Robert F. Wagner Labor Archives, New York University, Bobst Library.

Yeager, Matthew G. (2011) "Frank Tannenbaum: The Making of a Convict Criminologist," *The Prison Journal* 91(2): 177–197.

INDEX

Throughout this index, *f* indicates a figure on that page

Abramson, Esther (Mrs. Frank Tannenbaum) 35–6, 36*f*, 37*f*, 74
Adler Felix 83
Advertising Council 101
Alber, Louis 73
American Dilemma (Myrdal, 1944) 69
American Ethical Union of New York City 83
American Federation of Labor 8, 22
American League to Abolish Capital Punishment 103
American Prison Association 48, 76–7
The American Tradition in Foreign Policy (Tannenbaum, 1955) 102
anarchists, influences on Tannenbaum: Emma Goldman 6–7; IWW 8; Modern School of the Francisco Ferrer Association 7; Samuel Roth 7–8
Annual Governor's Conference (Illinois) 94
Army of the Unemployed 9–10, 11, 14
assaults, changes in Sing Sing and 44
Associated Press, on Tannenbaum's graduation 33
Atlantic Monthly, Tannenbaum's articles in 47–8, 57, 58–63
The Auburn Citizen 38
"Auburn model" penitentiary 60, 61
Auburn Penitentiary 40, 42–3, 49
authority, suspicion of 83–4

The Balance of Power in Society (Tannenbaum) 102
Barnes, Harry Elmer 92–3, 99, 103
Battle, George Gordon 47

Becker, Howard 89
bed bugs 28
Bell, Daniel 8
Belo, Jane (Mrs. Frank Tannenbaum) 96–7, 96*f*
Berkman, Alexander 12, 19, 34
Blackwell's Island Penitentiary: changes in after Tannenbaum's release 29–30; drawings of 23*f*, 25*f*, 26*f*, 29*f*; IWW members sent to 14; 1915 review of conditions in 27–8; Tannenbaum's descriptions of 20–1, 59, 61–2, 99; Tannenbaum's sentencing to 17; vagrants sent to 8
Brandeis, Alice 52
Brandeis, Louis 52
Brookings Institution 73
Brooklyn Institution 72
Brown, Thomas (Osborne's prison alias) 40, 40*f*
brutality in prison: documented by Tannenbaum for the Wickersham report 75–6, 77; history and universality of 59, 64–5; from regulation violations 59, 68; witnessed by Tannenbaum at Blackwells 26–7, 28; *see also* cruelty; punishment; torture in prison
bugs in prison 53, 61
"Butler Condemns College Bolsheviki" (*New York Times, 1917*) 35

Campbell, Magistrate 11
Canopus Hollow Farm 96

142

INDEX

capitalism: IWW views on 15; Tannenbaum as threat to 13, 17; Tannenbaum's views on 33, 34, 57–8

Capitalism and Slavery (Williams, 1944) 69, 101

capital punishment 56, 103

Carnegie Hall gathering to defend Osborne 46

Caron, Arthur 19

Carroll, Joseph D. 13

cell blocks 28, 29, 44, 52–3, 91

The Century Magazine 69–70, 72, 85

chain gang 69, 78

Chambliss, WIlliam 89

Charity Organization Society 31

Chicago Area Project 94

Chicago School of Sociology 88

Childs, Grace Hatch 30, 31

Childs, Richard S. 30

churches, Tannenbaum's view of obligations of 9–10, 67

class analysis 100

Clinton Penitentiary 57

"color line" 69–70

Columbia University: pressure to purge radical faculty 35; Tannenbaum as a lecturer at 79–80; Tannenbaum's activities in 32; Tannenbaum's conditional acceptance to 31–2; Tannenbaum's graduation from 32; Tannenbaum's tour of 30

Columbia University Press 93

Columbia University Seminar program 97

communication, escapism and 59

communism, Tannenbaum's views on 78–9, 101

community: convict 94; criminals as part of 68, 89; previous inmates in 94–5; suspicion of released convicts 54; using criminals as scapegoats 87

community interests, labor groups and 57–8

convict court 43–4, 45, 46, 51, 94; *see also* discipline; Mutual Welfare League (Sing Sing); self-government, prisoner; welfare leagues

convict criminology 98, 104, 105

convict-lease system 69

Cooper Union 45

Cornell University 79

corporal punishment 85

corruption in the penal system 53, 55, 89

Cressey, Donald 89, 103

Crime and the Community (Tannenbaum): background of 74–5, 83–6; "Dramatization of Evil" thesis in 89; influences in 49; overview of 87–91; reaction to 91–2; republishing of 93; Sutherland's critique of 86–7; translations of 71*n*1

crimes/criminals 20, 88, 90, 93; *see also* professional criminal, development of

criminal justice system *see* penal system

criminological theory, Tannenbaum's' contributions to 89, 90, 98

Criminology (Sutherland, 1924) 86

cruelty 59, 77; *see also* brutality in prison

Darker Phases of the South (Tannenbaum, 1924) 69

Davis, Commissioner 27

death penalty 56, 103

Debs, Eugene V. 58, 63

democracy, inmate *see* self-government, prisoner

detached gang worker model 96

Dewey, John 35, 103

The Diary of a Self-Made Convict (Hassler) 99

diesel therapy 64, 71*n*2

differential association 85

discipline: corporal 61; Osborne's ideas on 38, 42–4; reported in the Wickersham Commission report 75–6; typical 64–5; *see also* punishment

"Dramatization of Evil" thesis 89, 98

drugs: in Blackwell 26; charges in and recidivism 3; race and 3; in Sing Sing 45

Eastman, Max 18–19, 22, 24*n*6

education: as an important part of rehabilitation 103–4; as a positive pursuit 55; in Sing Sing 44; Tannenbaum's 30, 33, 103

"Education for Crime" (Tannenbaum presentation) 94, 95

Eldridge, Seba 86

Ellis, Havelock 60, 87

employment *see* work

equality 59–60, 70

escape attempts 44, 45, 59, 64

"Facing the Prison Problem" (Tannenbaum presentation) 62–3

Fackenthal, Frank D. 31–2

INDEX

Fair Competition pact 77
Ferrer y Guardia, Francisco 7
fine, Tannenbaum's, for unlawful
  assembly 17, 19
Flynn, Elizabeth Gurley 100
Foner, Philip 102
food/hunger: documented by
  Tannenbaum for the Wickersham
  report 75–6; in Sing Sing 43, 45;
  Tannenbaum's views on 9, 10, 72;
  unsafe 53; *see also* necessities of life
Frankfurter, Felix 75
Frankfurt School 70*n*1
Freedman, Teddy 14
Freschi, John 11

gangs 83–4, 85, 89, 95; *see also* street
  life
George Junior Republic 39
Ginn and Company 87
Goldman, Emma 6–7, 12, 18, 100
Good Conduct League (Auburn
  Penitentiary) 42–3
Gordon, Mary 84–5
government 57–8, 78
G.P. Putnam's Sons 32, 51–2
Grant, Jerry F. 33
group homes, development of the
  professional criminal and 83–4

habilitation efforts *see* rehabilitation,
  view of prison as
Hamilton, Frank 14
Harlem Casino celebration 21
Hart, Hastings 70
Harvard University Law School 75
Hassler, Alfred 99
Hayes, Carleton 30, 32
Hayes, Patrick 27, 29
Haywood, William D. 13
health care in prison: at Blackwell 28;
  impact of when released 54; lack of
  53, 62; in the southern prisons 69;
  Tannenbaum's call for 63
Holmes, Reverend 18
homelessness 8–9, 13, 18–19
home life, development of the
  professional criminal and 65, 68,
  83–4, 85
Horkheimer, Max 70*n*1
housing, for released prisoners 1, 54
Howard League 48
Hunt, George W. 70

Hurd, Richard M. 25
Hurwitz, Elaihu 74
Hurwitz, Sara Nessa (Tannenbaum)
  35–6, 37*f*
Hurwitz, Zalkind "Ziggy" (Tannenbaum)
  35–6, 37*f*, 74

idleness in prison 78
immigrants, development of gangs
  and 89
indeterminate sentence 63, 67
individual pathology model 75
Industrial Workers of the World (IWW):
  jailing leaders of 101; reaction to
  Tannenbaum arrest 12; Standard Oil
  strike and 22; Tannenbaum joining 8;
  Tannenbaum's disassociation with 78;
  Tannenbaum's principles from and
  prison life 27; Tannenbaum's views
  on 33–4
inmates *see* prisoners
Intercollegiate Socialist Society (ISC)
  32, 33
International Institute of Social Research
  70*n*1
Ironside 94
isolation: development of the
  professional criminal and 84, 89; after
  prison release 68–9; in prison 54,
  57, 59–60; Tannenbaum's articles on
  59–60; vicious circle of 57, 60

juvenile delinquency: home life
  and 83–4, 85; influences on 65;
  institutionalizing for as a contributor
  to continued crime 90, 92, 95–6;
  Tannenbaum's contribution
  to understanding 98; *see also*
  professional criminal, development of

Keppel, Frederick P. 30
Kincaid, Eugene 22–3
Kirchheimer, Otto 91
Kirchway, George W. 76
Kropotkin, Peter 7

labeling, development of the professional
  criminal and 85
labeling theory 68, 89, 96, 98, 103
labor in prison 61–2, 63, 77, 78; *see also*
  prison-made goods
labor movement, Tannenbaum's views
  on 57–8

INDEX

The Labor Movement: Its Conservative Functions and Social Consequences (Tannenbaum, 1921) 57–8
labor organizations, Tannenbaum's interest in 72–3
League of Labor and Political Prisoners 31
League of Women Voters 73
Lemert, Edwin 89, 103
letters, from convicts, Osborne's 50, 52, 53, 56n2
Lever Brothers 58
Lever, William H. (Lord Leverhulme) 58
Lewisburg Federal Penitentiary 99
Lewis, Ed 14
Lexington Avenue explosion 19
Lohman, Joseph 91
Lombroso, Cesare 60, 87, 90
Lombroso-Ferrero, Gina 60
Lowenthal, Max 75
Luhan, Mabel Dodge 22
The Lyric 7–8

mail in prison 54
"Man and His Institutions" (unpublished, Tannenbaum, 1957) 99
Manhattan House of Detention 18
The Masses (1914) 16, 18–19, 22, 25, 47–8
mass incarceration 3
Mattick, Hans W. 91–2, 98, 103
Matza, David 89
McKay, Commissioner 13
McKay, Henry 90
Mead, Margaret 96
mental illness, changes in Sing Sing and 44
Merrill, Michael 102
Merton, Robert King 103
Metro-Goldwyn-Mayer 56
The Mexican Agrarian Revolution (Tannenbaum, 1929) 73
Mills, C. Wright 101
minimum wage demands, Tannenbaum's 9
Mitchel, John Purroy 12
Modern School of the Francisco Ferrer Association 7
Morris, Ama 49
Mother Earth 6, 20
Moyer, Imogene 98
Municipal Lodging Home 8
Murton, Thomas 55–6
Mutual Welfare League (Sing Sing): development of 44–5; encouragement by Osborne for Tannenbaum to write about it 49; influence on Tannenbaum 55, 92, 103; superintendent ignoring 46; undermining of after Osborne's death 49; *see also* convict court; welfare leagues
Mydosch's Hall 22
My Life in Prison (Lowrie, 1912) 40
Myrdal, Gunnar 69

National Committee on Prison Labor 30
National Committee on Prisons and Prison Labor 60, 70, 92
National Recovery Administration 77
necessities of life: at Blackwell 28; Tannenbaum's views on 13, 14, 15, 20, 21; *see also* food/hunger
New Horizons in Criminology (Barnes and Tetters) 92
New School for Social Research 93
New York Call 13–14, 15, 17, 20, 34
New York Evening Post 10
New York Prison Association 48
New York State Prison Commission 25, 46, 57
New York State Prison Reform Commission 30, 40
New York Times: article on Columbia University 35; coverage of Tannenbaum's Army of the Unemployed 10, 11; coverage of Tannenbaum's trial 16; prison authority sources of 26; on Tannenbaum at a League of Labor event 31; Tannenbaum interview in (1951) 79; Tannenbaum's graduation and 33
New York Tribune 10, 46
New York World 10
nonintervention 96

O'Hare, Kate Richard 84
Ohio prison fire 76–7
The Ordeal of Thomas Mott Osborne see Osborne of Sing Sing (Tannenbaum, 1933)
"Osborne Must Go by Tuesday or Be Ousted" (*New York Tribune,* 1915) 46
Osborne of Sing Sing (Tannenbaum, 1933): development of 49–50; movie attempt of 56; overview of 52–6; President Roosevelt writing forward for 77; research for 50–1

145

INDEX

Osborne, Thomas Mott: assistance in Tannenbaum's acceptance to Columbia 30; background of 38–40; biography of 50; convict letters and questionnaires in possession of 50, 52, 53, 56*n*2; death of 49; dismissal of perjury case against 47; as a guest prisoner 40–1, 41*f*, 42, 56*n*1; indictment of 46–7; influencing Tannenbaum's view of equality in prisoners 60; prison reform attempts and opposition to 45–6, 55; prison reform movie produced by 56; after Sing Sing 47–8; at Sing Sing 40*f*; Tannenbaum's praise of 73, 94–5; views on crime 90

ostracization, development of the professional criminal and 84

Palmer raids 101
parole 63, 64, 67, 103
Peabody, George Foster 50
peer groups 45, 92
penal farms 67
Penal Institutions, Report No. 9 (1931) 52
penal system: as described by Tannenbaum 91; as described in *Osborne of Sing Sing* 52–3; expenditures of for corrections 4; Tannenbaum's vision of 63, 66, 94
penitentiaries *see* prison
perjury, Osborne indicted for 46
Perkins, Francis 10
A Philosophy of Labor (Tannenbaum, 1951) 102
"The Place for the Offender" (Tannenbaum presentation) 94
Plunkett, Charles Robert 15
police: discrepancies in reports on Tannenbaum's arrest 12–13, 17–18; press and 13, 17
Political Science Quarterly 78–9
politics: changes in Sing Sing and 45–6, 47, 49; Columbia University and radical faculty 35; crime and 90; prison reform and 48–9; Tannenbaum arrest and 12; Tannenbaum on the power of 101; Tannenbaum's acceptance to Columbia University and 31; Tannenbaum's call for 8 hour days and 13; Tannenbaum's later views on 79; Tannenbaum's orientation in 102; Tannenbaum trial and 17

Politics and Prisons (Osborne, unpublished) 48
Portsmouth Naval Prison 48, 56, 66
positive pursuits 55
Positivism 42, 44, 50, 59, 87–8
Post-Standard (Syracuse) 73
poverty, development of gangs and 89
President's Commission on Prison Industries 77
press: coverage of Tannenbaum trial 11–12, 13; editorial reaction to indictment of Osborne 46; impact of on Tannenbaum's arrest 11, 13, 17; impact on Osborne's work in Sing Sing 46; influence on police 13, 17
prison: aggravating the problem of crime 93; atmosphere of fear and hate in 54, 76; "Auburn model" 60, 61; beatings witnessed by Tannenbaum in 27; compared to slave plantations 3; conditions of in the Deep South 69–70; corruption in 53, 55, 89; isolation in 54, 57, 59–60; overall purpose of 64; prisoner correspondence about conditions of 53; riots witnessed by Tannenbaum 27–8; solitary confinement of Tannenbaum 27; Tannenbaum's allegations about 26; Tannenbaum's articles on cruelty in 58–60; Tannenbaum's suggested architecture of 66–7
Prison Association of New York 27, 45
prison brutality *see* brutality in prison
prison court *see* convict court
"Prison Cruelty" (*Atlantic Monthly*) 58–60
prisoners: creating a discipline committee in Auburn Penitentiary 42–3; incarcerated, rates of 1, 2*f*, 4*f*; jail as an institution for career criminals 92; lack of outside support system 3, 54–5; Osborne's views on after guest prisoner experience 42; race of 3; recidivism 2–3; refusing to testify against Osborne 46–7; released, rates of 1–2, 2*f*; social cohesion among 60; spirituality and 60, 66, 67–8, 69; Tannenbaum's suggestion for classification of 67–8
Prisoners Their Own Warders (McNair, 1899) 40
"Prison Facts" (*Atlantic Monthly*) 60–2
prison farms 62, 69

146

INDEX

Prison Industries Reorganization Administration 78

prison labor *see* labor in prison

Prison Labor Authority 77

prison-made goods 77–8; *see also* labor in prison

prison reform: American Prison Association meeting 76–7; contrast of systems in *Wall Shadows* 65; need for a national program 69; Osborne's attempts in and opposition to 55; Osborne's background and 39–40; Tannenbaum's speeches for 73, 75–6; Tannenbaum's views on 38, 57, 93; Tannenbaum's vision of 62–3; validity of Tannenbaum's ideas in 99; Virginia Institute of Public affairs address on 75; *see also* rehabilitation, view of prison as; Wickersham Commission

Prisons of the World (Cook, 1891) 40

professional criminal, development of: "Dramatization of Evil" thesis 89, 98; gang formation and 95–6; as opposed to an accidental offender 92; opposition to Tannenbaum's view on 87; overview of 65, 68; prison reform and 91; Tannenbaum's articles on 83–6; Tannenbaum's contribution to understanding 98; Tannenbaum's "psychological expectancy" 99–100; *see also* crimes/criminals; juvenile delinquency; recidivism

punishment: corporal 61, 85; current 64; for informing on prison conditions 53; not reducing number of crimes 93; for regulation violations 59, 68; Tannenbaum's documentation of types of 75; Tannenbaum's suggestions on 67; *see also* brutality in prison; discipline

Punishment and Social Structure (Rusche and Kirchheimer, 1939) 71*n*1

Putnam, George Palmer 32–3

race of prisoners 3, 69

Randall, John Herman 105*n*2

Rand School of Social Sciences 33

Rattigan, Charles 42

recidivism: peer contacts and habits contributing to 83; prisons contributing to 73–4, 86, 93, 99–100, 103; rates of 2–3; *see also* professional criminal, development of

Reconstructing Criminal Behavior (Tannenbaum) 86

regulation violations 59, 68

rehabilitation, view of prison as: idleness and 78; juvenile delinquency 95–6; reducing the role of the penal institution and 94; Tannenbaum's call for 62, 65–6, 74, 75, 93, 103; Tannenbaum's personal experience and 103–4; Tannenbaum's speech to the American Prison Association and 76–7; *see also* prison reform

reintegration of prisoners into the community 1–2, 68–9

religion 16, 20

Report on Penal Institutions, Probation and Parole (Wickersham Commission, 1931) 75

The Right Way (1921) 56

Riley, John 45–6

riots: aftermath of 77; discipline and 64; documented by Tannenbaum for the Wickersham report 75–6; idleness and 78; Tannenbaum accused of inciting 11, 13; Tannenbaum on 73–4; witnessed by Tannenbaum at Blackwells 26–7, 28

Robert Brookings Graduate School of Economics and Government 72

Rockefeller, John D. 19, 22

Roosevelt, Franklin D. 47, 51, 77

Roth, Samuel 7–8

rules *see* regulations violations

Russell Sage Foundation 70

Rutgers Square assembly 9, 12, 13, 17–18

The Saturday Evening Post 52

Schur, Edwin 89

Seager, Henry R. 58

self-government, prisoner 60, 65, 67; *see also* convict court; welfare leagues

Sellin, Thorsten 103

sentences, indeterminate 63, 67

sexual acts convictions at Sing Sing 46

Shaw, Clifford R. 90, 94

silent system 43, 53, 59

Sinclair, Upton 32

Sing Sing Penitentiary: changes in due to Osborne's changes 44–5; corruption in 43; inmates convicted for sexual acts in 46–7; inmates views of after reforms 66; Osborne and Tannenbaum

147

INDEX

at 40*f*; Osborne's improvements in 43–4; previous inmate testimony about 94–5; Tannenbaum's visit to 38, 39*f*, 40*f*, 47

The Slave and Citizen (Tannenbaum, 1947) 69–70

slave plantations, compared to U.S. penitentiaries 3

slavery 69, 70

social cohesion among prisoners 60

Socialism 57–8, 72, 79, 102

Social Science Research Counsel 50

solitary confinement 26, 27, 38

spirituality in prison 60, 66, 67–8, 69

St. Alphonsius Roman Catholic Church 11

The Standard 83, 84

Standard Oil Company 22

Standard Oil strike 22–3

Sterling Artists Bureau 73

Sternfeld, Julius 74

Stock Exchange Luncheon Club 6

"stool pigeon" system 43, 53, 54

street crime 65, 89, 92

street life 65, 83, 85, 95; *see also* gangs

strikes: at Blackwell 27, 28; Standard Oil 22–3; Tannenbaum's involvement in 21–2

suicide, changes in Sing Sing and 44

Sulfzer, William 40

Sutherland, Edwin H. 50–1, 85, 86–7

Swarthmore Chautauqua Association of Pennsylvania 73

syndicate crime 89

syphilis 69

Syracuse University 73

Tannenbaum, Abraham Wolfe 5

Tannenbaum crime: arrest 11–12; charges filed 14; discrepancies in 11–13; ending speeches at trial 16–17; reactions to conviction of unlawful assembly 17–18; release of 19–21; testimony filed in 15–16

"The Tannenbaum Crime" (*The Masses, May 1914*) 18–19

Tannenbaum, Esther (neé Abramson) 35–6, 36*f*, 37*f*, 74

Tannenbaum, Frank: changing views of 58, 72, 78–9, 100, 102; conceptions of the model prison 62–3; correspondence with Sutherland 51; doctorate topic chosen by 72–3; early working years 7–8;

early years 5–6; education 7; false arrest of during Standard Oil Strike 22–3; favorite photo of 104*f*; as the first convict criminologist 104; as guest prisoner in Sing Sing 47; homelessness and unemployment of 8–9; interest in Mexican labor organizations 72–3; involvement in IWW 8; at Sing Sing 39*f*, 40*f*; university photo 80*f*, 81*f*, 88*f*; U.S. Army experience 32; writing Osborne biography 50

Tannenbaum, Jane (neé Belo) 96–7, 96*f*

Tannenbaum, Louis 10*n*1

Tannenbaum, Sara Nessa (Hurwitz) 35–6, 37*f*

"Tannenbaum's articles: on Blackwell's Island" (*The Masses*, 1914) 25, 47–8; on the obligation of the Church toward prisoners 67; on prisons (*The Atlantic Monthly*) 47–8, 57, 58–63; on prisons in the Deep South (*Century Magazine*) 69–70; on prisons (*The Atlantic Monthly*) 47–8, 57, 58–63; on the professional criminal (*Century Magazine*) 85; on the professional criminal (*The Standard*) 83–4; response to coverage of his graduation (*The New York Times*) 33; response to perceived changing views (*New York Call*) 34; on vocational education and political prisoners 32; *Wall Shadows* 30, 63–7

Tannenbaum's letters 14, 18

Tannenbaum's speeches: to the American Prison Association 76–7; on arrest of IWW supporters 13; at Harlem Casino celebration 21; after release 19; Rutger's Square 9, 12, 13; Syracuse University 73; after trial 16; Union Square 21–2; the Virginia Institute of Public Affairs 75–6; at the "Youth and Community Service" (Illinois) 94–6

Tannenbaum trial: discrepancies in testimonies 12–13; IWW reaction to 12; politics in 12; remittance of fee 19–20

Tannenbaum, Zalkind (Hurwitz) 35–6, 37*f*, 74

teenage delinquency *see* juvenile delinquency

Thomas Y. Crowell Company 74, 86

148

INDEX

the Tombs 18

torture in prison: documented by Tannenbaum for the Wickersham report 75–6; Osborne film and 56; poor conditions constituting form of 45; prison discipline as 53, 69, 77; suffered by Tannenbaum 38; *see also* brutality in prison

tuberculosis 69

Ulman Commission 77, 78

Ulman, Joseph 77

unemployment 8–9, 13, 18–19, 21, 72, 89; *see also* work

unions, Tannenbaum's views on 58

University of Chicago Press 51

University of Kansas 86

University of North Carolina Press 52

unlawful assembly, Tannenbaum's conviction for 16

unsafe/unsanitary conditions in prison: in Blackwells 45, 61–2; documented by Tannenbaum for the Wickersham report 75–6; in the southern prisons 69; witnessed by Tannenbaum at Blackwells 26–7, 28, 38, 52–3

urban delinquency 89

U.S. Naval Prison 47, 48, 55

Veblen, Thorsten 103

violence *see* brutality in prison

Virginia Institute of Public 75

visitation 54, 64

Vold, George B. 93–4

voting, released prisoners and 1

Wadhams, William H. 16, 17, 19, 46

wages, paid in prison, Osborne's view of 45

Wall Shadows (Tannenbaum) 30, 63–7

wardens 61, 63, 66

War Labor Policies Board 32

Weeks, Frederick 38

welfare leagues 63, 65–6; *see also* convict court; Mutual Welfare League (Sing Sing); self-government, prisoner

Whitin, Fred (E. Stagg) 30

Whitman, Charles 46

Wickersham Commission 52, 75–7; *see also* prison reform

Wilder, Anna (Mrs. Abraham Tannenbaum) 5

Williams, Eric 69, 101

Wisotsky, Isidore 14–15

Within Prison Walls (Osborne, 1926) 42, 56

work: difficulties in obtaining after prison 54, 55, 68; outside of Sing Sing 47; prison-made goods 77–8; Tannenbaum's views on 72; *see also* unemployment

work day/wage demands, Tannenbaum's 9, 13

Yale University 79

"Youth and Community Service" conference 94

Youth Development Project 91